Fair Shares For All?

The Joseph Rowntree Foundation has supported this project as part of its programme of research and innovative development projects, which it hopes will be of value to policy makers and practitioners. The facts presented and the views expressed in this report, however, are those of the authors and not necessarily those of the Foundation.

Fair Shares For All?

Disparities in service provision for different
groups of people with learning difficulties
living in the community

by Carol Walker,
Tony Ryan and Alan Walker

RESEARCH *INTO* PRACTICE

RESEARCH *INTO* PRACTICE

Fair Shares For All?

**Disparities in service provision for different groups
of people with learning difficulties living in the community**

Carol Walker

Tony Ryan

Alan Walker

Published by:

Pavilion Publishing (Brighton) Ltd.

8 St George's Place

Brighton

East Sussex BN1 4GB

Telephone: 01273 623222

Fax: 01273 625526

Email: Pavpub@pavilion.co.uk

In association with the Joseph Rowntree Foundation.

First published 1996.

ISBN 1 900600 15 3

Editor: Anna McGrail

Cover, design and typesetting: Stanford Douglas

Printing: York Publishing Services

Contents

Acknowledgements

The research on which this report is based would not have been possible without the help and co-operation of those service users, their families and support staff, who agreed to be interviewed and take part. Many of the family respondents, in particular, led very busy lives; the time they gave and the patience they showed during the fieldwork was invaluable. We would particularly like to thank Alan Brooke, David Black and the Flaherty family.

We also received considerable help from many senior officers in the local authorities, NHS Trusts and voluntary and private agencies; they helped us draw the samples and contact respondents, as well as provide us with invaluable practical help and information throughout. Special thanks are due to Nick Morey, Phil Dand, Richard Cafeiro, Owen Cooper, Dennis Buckley, Elaine Gribbon, Mike Kelloway and all their colleagues.

We would also like to thank Bridget Costello, Andrew Fidler and Sue Roylance, who helped with the fieldwork, Margaret Jane, Chris Heatherinshaw and Jude Bennington for secretarial and administrative support, and Marg Walker, not least for her ability to translate the illegible into a coherent manuscript.

The project was funded by a generous grant from the Joseph Rowntree Foundation, for which we are grateful. Our sincere thanks are due to the members of the Advisory Group, who provided guidance throughout the project and, in particular, to Linda Ward for her support and advice. Finally, special thanks to Tom McLean for his continued commitment, both to our research and to the need for better opportunities and services for all people with learning difficulties. We hope this report contributes in some small measure towards the achievement of these goals.

Summary of Key Findings

This report examines the circumstances of 120 people living in the community in the North West of England, either with their families or in formal care. The main findings of the research include:

- People with learning difficulties living with their families receive very different levels and types of service provision from those living in group homes or being resettled from long-stay hospitals.

- People living in community placements have regular, individual support but limited access to community learning disability services. The situation for people living with their families is the reverse of this.

- People living in hospitals and hostels scheduled for closure receive priority consideration for community placements. Similar moves for those living with their families occur mainly in crisis situations when the caring relationship has broken down.

- Family carers reported that they needed higher levels and more flexible forms of support.

- Community living offers people with learning difficulties very considerable advantages over traditional institutional care, but further effort and resources are necessary to provide them with the further range of opportunities available to the rest of the community.

- Older people with learning difficulties (typically over 50) were offered fewer opportunities than younger people to develop personal skills, to take part in community activities and to develop social networks, even though they were likely to become more independent and develop skills.

Chapter One
Introduction

There have been a number of significant developments in ideas and practice concerning service provision for people with learning difficulties over the past two decades. Most importantly, there has been the philosophical shift in favour of the treatment of people with learning difficulties as individuals with human rights rather than as a sort of sub-species to be hidden away. This has led to a growing demand, both in the academic literature and in service-practice guidelines, to provide people with learning difficulties with the opportunity to live within and as part of local communities. As a result, concepts such as normalisation, social-role valorisation and the ordinary-life model have been widely, if not uncritically, accepted as appropriate goals for this previously neglected and stigmatised group of people. At the same time as this sea-change in ideas was taking place, the Conservative governments of the 1980s and early 1990s were promoting the concept of community care much more determinedly than their predecessors and, in particular, had introduced policies to accelerate the closure of long-stay hospitals, including those for people with learning difficulties. Both policies, in principle if not always in the detail, had cross-party support.

This shift in philosophical and policy orientation has profound implications for all people with learning difficulties: both those who have had, or who will have to learn to live outside the enclosed and segregated hospital setting and those already living in a range of different settings within the community — with their families, in hostels, in shared supported-housing or, less commonly, independently. Those in the former group have found themselves confronted with the many different challenges associated with a major change of lifestyle, and those in the latter have found agencies responsible for community-based services having to cope with new and additional demands created by the virtual abolition of long-term institutional care.

A number of studies have evaluated the movement of people out of long-stay institutions into the community. This work has provided important information on their experiences and has supported overwhelmingly the concept of community living, while still making clear the need for continuing improve-ment and development. Most of these studies have been of people who have moved out of institutions as part of an organised resettlement programme, some have concerned people who have benefited from the 'dowry' system whereby Regional Health Authorities release money in perpetuity to local service providers, either the local health district or local authority social services department, to cover the development of additional community services for people with learning difficulties. The adequacy of such payments has been called into question (Knapp *et al.*, 1992), however, there is no doubt that this system has allowed for the organised resettlement of people from hospital to the community with a prearranged package of care and, although research has shown that there is still room for further improvement in the implementation of the policy and in the quality and level of services provided (Collins, 1993; Walker, Ryan & Walker, 1993), in the main, closure of the mental handicap hospitals has not been accompanied by the same kind of disturbing examples of unsupported de-institutionalisation which have accompanied such closures in the psychiatric sector.

Background to the research

In 1982, the North Western Regional Health Authority (NWRHA) published *A Model District Service* (NWRHA, 1982), a strategy document which set out its plans for community provision for all people with learning difficulties in the Region. This included both an ambitious hospital closure programme, including three very large long-stay hospitals with over 2,900 beds and greater choice for people with learning difficulties not in formal care: 'On reaching adulthood both clients and families should have a choice as to whether the handicapped family member stays in the parental home or moves to a new home' (NWRHA, 1982).

Underlying *A Model District Service* was the principle of normalisation, and in particular the model of service provision developed by O'Brien (1985) in the 'five accomplishments'. Even when it came under increasing pressure because of the government-directed accelerated hospital-closure plan, the Region still maintained its commitment to user-centred resettlement.

An independent evaluation of the North West's resettlement programme, which was undertaken by the authors (Walker *et al.*, 1993), focused primarily on the outcomes for the people who were resettled. This report was cautiously optimistic: its main finding that resettlement presents people with a much higher quality of life than that permitted within a hospital setting was qualified by the need for the further development of community services, more staff training and greater opportunities for service users to exercise choice and to fully participate within a community.

That evaluation, which was completed in 1993, revealed two further issues which deserved exploration. The first, which was raised by many service providers, concerned the relatively advantaged position of people who had been resettled with funding into a planned programme of care in the community compared to those who had lived in the community longer term, either with their families or in formal care settings, such as hostels. The second issue concerned the emergence of a new group of service users, older people with learning difficulties, and the extent to which services were able and willing to recognise and adapt to their emergent needs.

Provision for different groups of people with learning difficulties living in the community

To qualify for NWRHA funding all care packages offered to the people moving out of hospital into the community had to meet minimum criteria which were based on the objectives of the Model District Service and which would maximise the opportunities for independent, integrated living. Most people moved into supported housing for three or four people. Formal service provision for people already living in the community has been more haphazard. For example, an evaluation project undertaken in the North West revealed that education and training was less satisfactory for those leaving hostels (without funding) than for those leaving hospitals (with funding) (Stenfert Kroese & Fleming, 1992). Intervention for people living with their families has tended to be even more limited and confined to crisis situations (Ward, 1990). This uneven access to and receipt of services led some user groups and community-based staff to express the fear that people with learning difficulties living with their families might be losing out. A report published by the NWRHA revealed a similar concern: 'In conclusion, for people with moderate learning difficulties there is a shortage of good quality accommodation and of the appropriate supports to enable people to make a success of home life, especially for those who have not been residents of institutions at some stage, that is for people for whom service organisations may have little incentive to provide options' (NWRHA, 1991, p 45).

Older people with learning difficulties

Considerable attention has been paid to the ageing of the general population, however, until relatively recently the implications of this for older people with learning difficulties, their informal carers and service providers received little attention in the UK. This gap in knowledge is due, at least in part, to the fact that the increased longevity of this group of people is a welcome demographic change. The Department of Health estimated that, in 1991, 47% of people with learning difficulties in the care of District Health Authorities were 45 or over and 17% were 65 or over. The closure of the long-stay hospitals will mean that more older people with learning difficulties will live in the community and will therefore need community service support. In the NWRHA resettlement study, over two-fifths of the people who had moved out of hospital were 50 or above at the time of resettlement. Even so, the average age of those resettled was lower than the average age of those in hospital.

The growing numbers of people with learning difficulties who live into older age present dilemmas and challenges for the traditional models of service delivery which tend to be fragmented. Thus, services for those with learning difficulties have not geared themselves towards the needs of these people as they get older; similarly services for older people have not normally accepted, within their remit, older people with learning difficulties.

Models of service delivery and service provision

The ultimate aim of *A Model District Service* was to establish a comprehensive, community-based service for all people with learning difficulties. There are, however, several barriers in the way of the realisation of this goal. It requires close working between Regional and District health authorities, as well as with social services agencies. There is a need to reconcile different staffing structures and philosophies as well as different financial management systems. The goal of 'seamless' provision for all people with learning difficulties in the Region, whether or not they have been in the long-stay hospitals, conflicts with the requirement to ring fence resettlement monies 'in perpetuity' (NWRHA, 1982).

The growing number of older people with learning difficulties living in and moving into the community, an increasing proportion of whom will have outlived their family carers, poses new challenges for the providers of services for older people as well as for those providing services for people with learning difficulties. Although the needs of all people tend to increase as they reach advanced old age, the age discrimination inherent in some aspects of service delivery means that these needs are less, rather than more, likely to be met. Older people with learning difficulties face 'double jeopardy' (Sweeney & Wilson, 1979;

Hogg *et al.*, 1988; Walker *et al.*, 1996) if their needs are not adequately acknowledged either by services for people with learning difficulties or by services for older people. In the past it has been assumed that older people with learning difficulties should receive the same services as other older people (Social Services Committee, 1985) but there are serious problems associated with this approach. On the one hand, people with learning difficulties may be given entirely inappropriate services by, for example, grouping them together with those suffering from Alzheimer's and, on the other, there is the risk that the specific needs of this group or sub-groups among it become submerged by those of the much larger group of older people and, thereby, become invisible. The existence of specific community services for all older people means that there is greater potential for those with learning difficulties to integrate. However, if this is done, it needs to be managed carefully to avoid the danger of treating older people's services as ghettos for those whom the wider community would prefer to ignore.

The implementation of the *National Health Service and Community Care Act* (1990) has increased both the opportunities and threats to services for people with learning difficulties. On the one hand, it offers service users the opportunity to have their needs assessed. On the other hand, experience of implementing the legislation in some local authorities and district health services has revealed a lack of resources to meet all of the needs that have been identified. This brings into question how far service providers can cope with the as yet unidentified needs of others, such as people with learning difficulties living with their families. The introduction of the purchaser/provider split in service provision offers similar challenges, especially with respect to joint collaboration between different service sectors and different providers which are not yet being met by joint commissioning.

The aims of the research

This report is based on recent research, funded by the Joseph Rowntree Foundation, which looked at the circumstances of different groups of people with learning difficulties living in the community. In ***Chapters Two*** and ***Three*** we examine and compare the experiences and quality of life of people with learning difficulties who have been resettled *within* the community (either from the family home or hostels) to those who have been resettled from long-stay hospitals in the North Western Regional Health Authority and others who are still living with the family. In ***Chapter Four*** we explore the specific needs of, and the nature and quality of services provided for, older people with learning difficulties.* In the ***Conclusion*** (***Chapter Five***) we examine the policy context within which learning difficulty services operate in the North West.

Research methodology

The research was based in five Health Districts within the NWRHA, all of which had been involved in the earlier research project conducted by the research team. The local authorities reflected different models of service delivery. Three of the authorities chosen had integrated services for people who had been relocated from hospital into their general learning-disability service, though in one the resettlement dowry was kept separate for use by this group. The other two authorities had kept service provision for people who had been resettled from hospital separate, though in one case part of the income from the dowries had been allocated to general learning-disability services. (For further information on the composition of the sample see ***Appendix Two***.)

---

* The research project led to the creation of a European network of people working in the field of older people with learning difficulties, ENIDA (European Network on Intellectual Disabilities and Ageing); see ***Appendix One***.

The sample was structured to include 60 people who had been resettled from hospital and 60 who had lived in the community longer term. We then subdivided each group by age so that approximately half would be over and half under the age of 50. Sixty-two of the people who had been included in our previous study had been relocated to the five areas. Of these, two had died. All the remaining 60 were contacted through their service providers and agreed to take part. Where possible, permission was obtained from the individual concerned. Where there was little communication, permission was sought through a care worker or Individual Programme Plan (IPP) group. Throughout this report this group is referred to as the 'ex-hospital' group. The other sample of 60 people was drawn from records held by local authority social services departments, such as local registers for people with learning difficulties and records of people living in supported living schemes. Half had moved into shared housing from other community settings: 18 from hostels, six from the family home and six from other independent provision. This group is referred to as the 'community group'. The other 30 people in this part of the sample were still living with their families: the 'family group'. It should be noted that all those identified in the family group were either currently or in the past had been in contact with the statutory services. It is known that there are considerable numbers of people with learning difficulties living in community settings who do not have any such contact (Hogg *et al.*, 1988). Participation of the people with learning difficulties living with their families was primarily dependent on the co-operation of the family carer because we could only gain access through them. The role of the family carer as gatekeeper is discussed later in this report.

All the people in the ex-hospital group were white; this reflects the ethnic composition of the populations of the hospitals concerned.

The community sample could not be structured by ethnic group because the local authority records did not record this information. As a consequence there were only two non-white service users in the sample — one living in supported accommodation and one living with his mother — even though the study included areas with sizeable ethnic minority populations. It is likely that people with learning difficulties in ethnic minorities are under-represented in social services records and it is known this is the case in other related areas of service provision (Fatimelehin & Nadirshaw, 1994). Some work is being undertaken in Oldham and Rochdale to examine the issue of race and learning difficulty.

A main focus of the research process was to maximise the input from people with learning difficulties themselves. However, the sample of service users covered a broad spectrum of competence and disability (see *Appendix Two*). In particular, because of the wide variation in communication skills, there was a significant number from whom it was not possible to obtain any information directly. All the respondents with learning difficulties were approached. Unstructured interviews, guided by an *aide memoire*, and/or group interviews, were carried out with 37 people (14 in the ex-hospital group, 15 in the community group and eight in the family group). The group interviews, with between two and five people at a time, were very successful as the participants seemed to gain confidence from being part of a group.

It is more problematic to obtain the views of people with learning difficulties with little or no communication skills in research of this kind. Previous work has shown that using visual techniques, such as photographs and symbols, can be helpful (Walker *et al.*, 1993; Booth *et al.*, 1990; Conroy & Bradley, 1985). However, such techniques are most useful where the respondent is being asked to choose between different preferences, for example, choosing between different living situations. In this study there was no concrete central question which lent itself to visual representation. As a result, the views of people with learning difficulties presented in this report represent only those who were able to communicate verbally. Honestly representing the views of service users with no or little communication is a serious issue for researchers but also, perhaps more importantly, for planners, commissioners, carers and service providers. It is important neither to underestimate nor to over-estimate the extent to which people with learning difficulties are

able to express their views. There will always be a group of people who are not able to express their views in ways which others can understand. Researchers and service providers have to explore ways in which those who represent them put their apparent needs to the fore in any planning processes. At the very least this will involve a commitment of time and contact which is not possible within research of this scale and duration.

Interviews were also conducted with the person's carer: the care worker of those living in formal settings (90) and the family carer for those living at home (30). A structured interview was undertaken with the former but not the latter. After the pilot stage the structured questionnaire for family carers was abandoned in favour of a less structured approach which was more flexible to individual circumstances and concerns. This was underpinned by a greatly abridged questionnaire which recorded a number of standard indicators. Finally, 42 of the people resettled from hospital were in close contact with a relative. Of these, 27 agreed to be interviewed.

Quality of life

The main aim of the research was to compare the quality of life of different groups of people with learning difficulties living in the community. In keeping with the earlier discussion, there were two main sets of comparisons made. First, to compare quality of life and service provision of people living in different care settings in the community: those resettled, with funding, from hospital; those resettled, usually without funding, from hostels or the family home; and those still living in the family home. The second basis for comparison rested on age. The age of 50 was adopted to denote the start of older age, because this is the point at which the third age is commonly said to begin. In both cases the reference point for measuring quality of life was *not* institutional living, which other studies have found offer a limited and restricted lifestyle (Emerson & Hatton, 1994) but the ordinary lifestyle available to the wider community.

Measuring quality of life is fraught with difficulty. It has been said that there are as many quality-of-life definitions as there are people (Liu, 1976). A review of 80 quality-of-life scales found little agreement between the authors (Felce & Perry, 1995). However, although it is proving difficult to agree an objective definition, there is general agreement on five areas which contribute to an individual's quality of life: physical well-being, social well-being, material well-being, development and activity, and emotional well-being (Felce & Perry, 1995). Each of these subsumes a total of 32 subsidiary headings. It would be very complex, therefore, to put such a model fully into operation.

In this study, we concentrated on three areas which broadly fall under the headings of material and social well-being and development and activity. These are consistent with the model of the 'five accomplishments' and 'ordinary life model' on which policy in the North West drew. Both centre around the need to enable individuals not only to live in but to be fully integrated within their local communities and to provide them with opportunities to be involved in decisions which affect their everyday lives. This philosophy can be equated with the notion of autonomy which Doyal and Gough (1991, p.54) have defined as being, along with physical health, the basic human needs: 'physical survival and personal autonomy are the preconditions for any individual action in any culture, they constitute the most basic human needs — those which must be satisfied to some degree before actors can effectively participate in their form of life to achieve any other valued goals'.

However, autonomy is denied to the majority of people with learning difficulties. By virtue of their social status and the response of society to their disability, they are not rewarded as they get older with greater control over their own actions. They are often treated as perpetual children with others making decisions on their behalf. While the normalisation model has been criticised for making people with learning difficulties fit into an unwelcoming and discriminatory society rather than expecting society to adapt to the diverse needs of all its members, it has been influential in helping to put the service user at the centre of the debate, arguing that users, regardless of their level of disability, should be encouraged and enabled to participate as far as possible in the organisation of their everyday lives.

Doyal and Gough (1991) assert that the basic needs of disempowered groups are no different to those of anyone else, however, they need 'additional and specific satisfiers' to address the 'additional threats to their health and autonomy' with which they are faced. This is particularly relevant for people with learning difficulties, as consideration of the three

prerequisites for individual autonomy — **understanding**, **cognitive/emotional capacity** and **opportunity** — shows. In all three respects, people with learning difficulties are disadvantaged or excluded. According to Doyal and Gough (1991, p63), understanding is dependent on effective teaching and learning from others. If not taught or if badly taught, the individual is 'objectively disabled'. Cognitive/emotional capacity, they argue, is dependent on a number of factors including the intellectual capability to formulate aims, the confidence to want to act and to participate in everyday life, and an understanding of the constraints on the success of their actions — none of which can be automatically assumed of people with learning difficulties. Opportunity is dependent on meaningful choices and the range of opportunities for significant action — again something which can never be taken for granted with regard to this group of people. In considering the quality of life of people with learning difficulties and in particular the degree of autonomy which they possess, it is important to consider whether the failure to enable them to meet their full potential in relation to understanding, cognitive/emotional capacity and opportunity is a result of their own developmental disability or whether it is socially constructed.

Objective measures have their limitations and dangers. Most importantly, they inevitably give the 'professional' or 'expert' the lead role, at the expense of the actual wishes of service users. They are also usually service- and resource-led which can lead to under-representing and under-recording of real need and can reproduce stereotyping of user groups, especially with regard to gender, race, age or even disability. The construction of appropriate subjective measures is always contentious but is particularly so for people with learning difficulties, first because of the limited or complete lack of communication skills of a significant proportion and secondly because of the segregated and disempowered lifestyles of the majority — regardless of their physical setting.

As Felce and Perry (1995) point out: 'Obtaining an answer is a necessary but not sufficient condition of sound interviewing'. For the reasons discussed earlier, any subjective assessment made by the learning disabled person may be problematic because of their limited life experience, because of frequent acquiescence when in situations of authority and because of limited comprehension or communication. However, relying on information from a third party is also problematic. If they know the person well then they are not disinterested; if they do not, then they are even less likely to be able to represent their views accurately. Felce and Perry (1995) argue that any third party should share key characteristics, such as age, gender, race and shared experience. In the research reported here, we could obtain information only from those people who were involved: namely the service user where possible and the person closest to them, in all cases a family carer or care worker. Any shared characteristics between the two would have been quite coincidental. In order to minimise the problem, we endeavour here to present the views of both users and carers straightforwardly and honestly, neither minimising nor exaggerating the information obtained. The names of those who took part have been changed to preserve their anonymity.

Chapter Two
Fair Shares For All?

The move from institutional to community forms of provision, not surprisingly, has led to an increase in the number of people with learning difficulties living in community settings; it has also raised the profile of the needs of this group of service users, including those already living in community settings. Community health and social services now have to cater for the needs of people whose access to and need for such services varies widely. The strategy adopted by the North Western Regional Health Authority (NWRHA) proposed combined services for all people with learning difficulties. In practice, this is a long-term objective which involves challenging traditional practices and priorities. In addition, the run-down and closure of the long-stay mental-handicap hospitals meant that, in the short term at least, priority was given to those being relocated. The bulk of the resources transferred from the RHA to the receiving services was tied to the individual being relocated; these monies could only be used to bolster community provision for other people with learning difficulties living in the community, as they were freed up on the death of those who had been relocated or those who were still living in the hospitals prior to closure. The new packages of care being provided for people moving out of hospital, funded by the dispersal of health resources, contrasted sharply with the growing 'care gap' in local authority provision (Walker, 1985) between rising needs in the community and the public resources allocated to meet them. This inevitably led to some concern among Regional policy-makers, care workers and informal carers, that the variation in funding according to service background, together with the concentration of resources and effort on getting people out of the long-stay hospitals, was creating inequalities in the formal support and care services provided, with ex-hospital residents getting the 'Rolls-Royce' service (NWRHA, 1992; Collins, 1993; House of Commons Health and Social Services Committee, 1985).

The provision of services to all people with learning difficulties on a basis which is seen to be fair and equitable presents a major challenge to service providers. Our research set out to examine how far they achieved this. We looked at the circumstances of three groups: those who had been resettled from long-stay institutions with funding; those who had been resettled within the community from hostels or the family home to more independent settings, without new funding; and those who were still living with an informal carer, in most cases with a family member.

This chapter considers the adequacy and equity of service provision for the three groups living in community settings. The following chapter then examines the outcomes for them with a view to evaluating and comparing their quality of life.

The need for care versus support

People with learning difficulties are not a homogeneous group. They vary widely in their levels of physical and developmental abilities and disabilities. The problems they face in their everyday lives are compounded by the stigma that they have suffered and, for large numbers, by their enforced social and economic exclusion from the wider community. The kind of assistance that people with learning difficulties require therefore varies widely. Some people with severe learning difficulties need physical *care*, that is, they need others to undertake tasks on their behalf, including personal care needs, or cooking and preparation for meals (Qureshi & Walker, 1989). In this sense, care is something that is usually done *to* the recipient both in terms of 'tending' with physical needs and, especially but not only by informal carers, with emotional needs. Other people with learning difficulties may not need assistance with physical tasks but, either because of their level of competence or because of restricted opportunities in the past, may require only **support**, that is, the assistance of others to help them to do things for themselves. This may involve helping them to gain **confidence** and then giving them the **opportunity** to do things for themselves, such as routine self-care tasks, household tasks, making decisions and participating in activities in the community. Support, in this sense, is conceived of in ideal terms as a process of empowerment. This means that different levels of support should be offered to people depending on their competence and will vary over time as abilities change, an approach which demands a high level of skill on the part of support workers. In practice, the assistance rendered to people with learning difficulties, both informal and formal, often takes the form of care when it should be support.

The dominant service philosophy applied to people with learning difficulties is based on the ideal of helping the individual to obtain the highest possible level of independence and integration. Maintaining the correct balance between care and support is a crucial variable in achieving this. Insufficient care can undermine the individual's quality of life and can restrict activities for which he or she needs only support. Care, when given unnecessarily, can create dependency (Walker, 1981, 1982). If insufficient or inappropriate support is available, then the individual will not be able to obtain and/or maintain control over important aspects of daily living. Conversely, too much or the wrong type of support may limit the individual's self-determination by being over-protective and thus fostering dependence rather than independence.

Profile: Susan Claridge

Susan Claridge lives in a small block of sheltered flats. There are five flats in all with a full-time support worker on hand. All those who live there have been resettled from long-stay hospitals. Susan herself is blind but copes very well for much of the day. She does need some help in preparing meals and going out. Much of the time she likes to listen to plays on Radio Four. However, Susan also has the biggest flat in the complex and it is therefore the flat that social services have chosen to house the support worker and administrative base. The result is that support workers tend to spend a lot of time in the flat and Susan has virtually 24-hour care, which she clearly does not need. Support workers recognise this and feel uncomfortable with the situation. The situation does not lend itself well to the encouragement of a feeling, for Susan, that it is her home. When asked whom she thought was the most important person in the flat she answered:

'Well I don't know how to answer that one, I don't know. I know it's not me'.

The determination of an appropriate level of formal care and/or support rests on a number of complex factors, including the needs of the individual, the needs of other people with whom he or she is living, the availability of community provision and the priority given to different types of assistance available to different groups of service users.

Living in formal care

It follows from the above discussion that it is not only the quantity of care and support offered which is important, but its nature and appropriateness to the needs of the service user. The most common model of formal care provided to people with learning difficulties today is shared, supported accommodation. Most people in our sample were living in three- or four-bedded placements, with 24-hour staff cover. In theory, this should provide service users with care and support which is appropriate to their individual needs and geared towards individual goals. In hospitals or in the traditional residential care homes, in which a few older people in our sample lived, the needs of the individual are often subordinated to the needs of the group and services are provided on a group basis. Consequently, priority tends to centre on, and often to end with, the physical care of the residents, thus reinforcing a culture of dependence.

Staffing

The level of staffing and the nature of the support and/or care provided has important implications for the level of independence and autonomy achieved by the service user. Overall, people who had been resettled from hospital had higher levels of staffing than those who had been resettled from elsewhere (see *Table 2.1*).

Not only were there differences in the numbers of staff who worked with the two groups, but there were also some differences in the status and qualifications of the staff themselves. The people in the community group who lived in supported housing were more likely to be supported by trained, qualified staff. However, those working with the ex-hospital group tended to be employed in more junior positions and they also had less experience. Three-quarters of the staff working with the ex-hospital group were employed as direct care or support workers, care assistants or residential social workers. The remainder were more senior workers, such as homeleaders and senior residential workers. The staff working with the community group tended to be more diverse than this. Half were employed as care assistants or residential workers and the remainder were

Table 2.1 **Staff/Resident Ratios***

	Ex-hospital	Community
High	31.7	23.3
Medium	50.0	26.7
Low**	13.3	46.7
Don't Know	5.0	3.3
Total number	60.0	30.0

*   High staffing = 1:1; medium = 1:2; low = 1: 3 or more.
** Includes people living in residential/nursing homes, warden-controlled settings and living independently with supervision.

in more senior positions, including community learning-difficulty nurses and social workers. In the light of our discussion of care versus support, it is noteworthy that the job title, care assistant as opposed to support worker, did not imply any difference in the kind of help they were expected to give service users: in essence, the roles were exactly the same. In this report, we generally use the term 'care worker' to describe those working with the people in our sample as this is the title used by employers. In many respects it also best describes what the workers actually do. However, we agree with many organisations of, or representing, people with learning difficulties who prefer the term 'support worker' because it puts the autonomy of the service user to the fore. The problem of nomenclature we faced was that, for the most part, many staff were not operating as support workers in the empowering sense prescribed by these organisations and as we have defined it earlier.

Training

Our previous research (Walker *et al.*, 1993) in the North West on the resettlement of people from long-stay institutions to supported living in the community, expressed concern that, though the Region's philosophy was based on enabling each individual person with a learning difficulty to maximise their own autonomy and independence, in practice this might be hampered by lack of staff or, just as significantly, by a lack of training. As a consequence care workers often did not understand that their primary role was to foster independence, not merely to care for or contain the service user. At the same time some care workers themselves identified the need for more and well-targeted training to enable them to perform the difficult task of supporting autonomy.

In our latest study, just over half the care workers of those in the community group and only one-third of those in the ex-hospital group, thought that their training had been good. Roughly a quarter in each group thought it was adequate and one-in-eight and one-in-three respectively thought it was poor. Staff employed by health districts and social services tended to have had similar levels of training, while those working in private and non-profit organisations tended to have received less. Training for those working with the community group tended to concentrate on personal care tasks, while those working with the ex-hospital group had had more varied training, such as in personal relationships and sexuality, HIV and AIDS, transition after resettlement, and mental health problems for people with learning difficulties.

Training is particularly important given the backgrounds of the care workers. Two-thirds of the staff working with the ex-hospital group had no formal qualification for the job, compared to just under half of those working with people in the community group. This is partly attributable to the proximity of each area to the hospitals from which people were discharged. For example, the district with the lowest proportion of trained staff was situated near to the hospitals and tended to recruit from untrained but experienced ex-hospital staff. Districts further away had to draw on less experienced, but perhaps more qualified, personnel. Most of the care workers who have experience of working with people with learning difficulties gained it in institutional settings. Consequently, they too need training once they move into a community setting to help them to recognise the very different model of care which should be applied.

Living with the family

The primary responsibility for the care of people living in informal care settings falls to the informal carer, normally a relative.

In the extensive literature on informal care, it is common for these responsibilities to be described as 'burdens' and, of course, in objective terms, caring often entails physical, emotional and financial strains (Twigg, Atkin & Perring, 1990; Glendinning, 1992). However, there is no doubt that many informal carers we spoke to derived great satisfaction from their role: a response which has been found in other studies of the informal carers of people with learning difficulties (Grant & Nolan, 1993). A common theme that emerges from this group of carers, which was identified also by relatives who had placed their learning-disabled relative into institutional care, was a strongly felt sense of duty. Parents especially stressed that their adult child was their responsibility because they had brought them into the world. However, parents were often reluctant to pass this obligation on to another family member, such as a sibling, because of the very great sacrifices involved. Therefore, informal care was not experienced purely as a burden nor solely as a source of satisfaction but a mixture of both.

The circumstances of informal carers are of course quite different from those who are paid to do the job in the formal sector. First, they do not have agreed contract hours, and they have to provide cover 24-hours a day and seven days a week; they do not have annual holiday entitlements or sick leave. Secondly, they may be financially disadvantaged because their participation in the labour market is often restricted or curtailed by their caring responsibilities. Thirdly, they are not paid — beyond possibly the modest limits of the invalid care allowance. Twelve of the 30 people included in the family group lived with a lone parent. Six carers had more than one person with either a learning difficulty or other disability to care for. In addition, six carers reported that they themselves had a disability or serious health problem which affected their ability to give support.

Profile: Mrs Humphries

Many years ago, Mrs Humphries adopted two young men with severe learning difficulties. It was a decision which she says has brought her great joy and satisfaction over the years. The oldest of the two, Peter, is now 24, the other is 14. Mrs Humphries now has a legacy from her previous occupation as a PE teacher, an increasingly painful and disabling knee complaint. She has been told that her mobility will steadily decrease. His mother's increasing mobility problem has meant that Mrs Humphries has not been able to take Peter out as much as she would have wished to, and they now spend much of their time confined to the house and garden. Mrs Humphries does get some help from friends who take Peter out occasionally. She also has a break when he goes to a respite care facility for five weeks a year, which he enjoys. Both Mrs Humphries and those who know her believe it is time for Peter to move on to his own place. The local authority is aware of her problem and plans are being made to enable Peter to live more independently of his mother. In Mrs Humphies' eyes, it is probably about time Peter moved on, just like any other young person of his age.

Despite the satisfaction often reported, for some of the family carers in the study the task of caring could be a formidable one. This was particularly true for those looking after adults with complex disabilities. Three people with learning difficulties in the family group also had severe physical disabilities and were unable to undertake personal care tasks. Eight people were said to display challenging behaviour of some kind, including two who were self-injurious. Four sets of carers were frequently woken during the night:

'I mean I go to bed at night and I don't know how many times I'm going to get up or whether I'm going to get a night's sleep, er... invariably it's six o'clock in the morning and I have to get up and see to her and she is very, very demanding.'

'But it's the monotony with Phillip, it's the same old thing every day. Before you can do anything for yourself, it's like an hour in the morning. That's the first thing then teatime is the same, and it's every single day.'

The responsibility for care usually fell to one or two individuals in the family. Family carers received help from close relatives in less than one-quarter of cases (23.3%); even fewer received any assistance from friends or members of the local community (16.7%). In some cases, the family carer did not seek such support because they did not wish to impose their 'burden' on anyone else.

Help from others

Despite the very heavy responsibilities family carers were carrying, with very little help from other family members or members of their local communities, only a minority had any close link with formal services. Although all the people in the family sample had been drawn from the official records of either the district health authority or the local social services department only two in five had regular contact with a social worker or community nurse.

The attitudes of carers towards the service offered by professionals were mixed. In three cases, it was reported that all they did was to organise respite care. One carer, who preferred to deal with the respite service direct, was unhappy with the recent change in policy, which meant that placements could only be made through a keyworker. Four families were getting advice about options for future housing

and support and one family was getting advice on a programme for challenging behaviour. In one case the family contact with the social worker had recently diminished because her main involvement had been to arrange travel assistance to help the family get to meetings. When the father retired, this outside assistance was no longer needed. None received any regular domiciliary support.

Support workers

For those who were in regular contact with a support worker, there were obvious benefits, which were acknowledged in the very positive attitudes expressed by some of the carers:

'Ricky (community nurse) is very good... If you've got a problem, you can ask and you can talk to him, but there must be a load of other people so he must have to spread himself fairly wide. I think if there were more people available like Ricky then that would help.'

'I can talk to her, sort things out with her, discuss everything with her and then we come to some kind of agreement. She's great.'

The relationship between informal carer and professional is a very personal one and varies, among other things, according to how well the individuals get on together. Families reported different qualities of relationships with different key workers over time and, as in the following example, found ways of bypassing those whom they did not find effective.

'I have to admit that my association with social workers hasn't been very good. The social workers that I have had have been useless, less than useless, more of an irritant than anything. I have found that if I need anything then I ring Jack [senior social worker] who is excellent and very helpful and very supportive.'

The main and often the only form of practical help given to family carers was the provision of a day centre place. For these people, the day centre manager, not the key worker, was the main point of contact with the formal care sector. Twenty-one of those who used formal day provision also had keyworkers whose job it was to co-ordinate Individual Programme Plan (IPP) meetings which took place infrequently and they had very little involvement with them otherwise. The contact that family carers had with key workers was limited almost entirely to IPP meetings.

Respite care

After day-centre places, the main service received by those living with their families was respite care, in fact this service is almost exclusively used by this group. As well as providing the learning disabled person with an opportunity to spend time away from home, respite care provides family carers with an essential break from their caring responsibilities; many said they would find it difficult to continue without it. Two-thirds (63.3%, n=19) of the families in the study said they currently had access to some form of respite care. Over half (56.7%, n=17) used local authority, privately-owned or NHS Trust provision which was based on ordinary living models of care which suited all but one of the unpaid carers. Two people spent time away from home with relatives, two went into an older persons' home. In another two cases a care worker came to stay in the family home and one person went into a family placement. Hostel-based respite care was used by three people. One family carer did comment on this: 'It isn't a super place, it's what I call a "loving dump", and Sue is quite happy there and content... I mean, these people are used to living in ordinary housing with decent living accommodation and that's what we want it [respite care] to be. Whereas [the hostel] is a

hostel and no matter how good the staff are, it's still a hostel and there are a lot of people milling around doing their own thing.'

Service deterioration

The main criticisms of respite care made by relatives were that there was not enough of it and, secondly, that it was extremely inflexible. Access to respite care varied. Those who did use it generally got a block of four or five weeks. Families also sometimes could get the occasional weekend. Six of the carers who used residential respite care said that they would have liked to have more provision but availability had in fact become tighter. After the closure of one unit, one carer commented: 'At one stage there was the Bowness Centre, there was facilities that would cater for the weekend. You knew you could book Ron in there and it would be virtually guaranteed that you could get him in. But now this facility has been closed down and the guarantee is not there.'

When asked how often they used the service, another carer added: 'Whenever they can fit her in. Because it's gone worse, it's such an overused service. It's gone worse, absolutely worse.'

The following family carers had been impressed when their daughter initially used respite provision but they had found that the quality of service had deteriorated recently: 'We don't think they do as much with her now as they used to do. It's the money and more people using the place you see. They used to ring up and they used to have a key worker. They used to come round and talk to us, you see. Well, that's all gone by the board now. And the other thing they used to do was take her to Camelot [a theme park], you know, and... she used to thoroughly enjoy that... That has all stopped now.'

Another family carer was at the point of exasperation at the lack of provision. Her daughter wakes during the night so she can only get an unbroken night's sleep when her daughter is away. 'Short-term care, I don't think there's enough. I mean sixteen beds in [local authority], I think that's horrendous! I mean, how many people with learning difficulties are there in [local authority]? We asked for a weekend in November and it just came back, "Sorry, full." That's it — you just don't get it... We need three Alcock Streets [respite facility].'

Lack of flexibility

The second major problem identified by family carers was the lack of flexibility in the respite-care system which made it difficult for families to make plans. For example, it often proved very difficult for families to book a holiday and arrange respite care for the relevant period. 'You don't know whether to book your holiday and then try and book Sandra in, or get Sandra into Pennine House and then book your holiday. Whichever way round you do it, it never works out.'

The domiciliary respite services were similarly inflexible. Paid carers usually came for the same hours each week during which time family carers felt compelled to do something regard-less of the circumstances. As one man put it: 'Sometimes you get the carers coming in and it's been raining. Sometimes I think it's been a waste of time getting them in. We've stayed in a few times with them, when it's been really torrential, you don't want to go out in that, do you?'

The holiday period presents the biggest challenge to service providers because of a natural surge in demand for respite care. One local authority has tried to accommodate this by using community care money to commission a new voluntary organisation to organise holidays for people with learning difficulties. In this way, both the family carer and the person with learning difficulties get a holiday. Although the authority recognises that there will always be a demand for permanent residential respite provision, it hopes that the success of the new service will encourage service users to use this more leisure-based provision.

The overload on respite services was acknowledged by the purchasers in all the districts we covered. Family placement and voluntary schemes were being developed partly to provide service users with more choice but also because they are cheaper forms of respite care. Three authorities were using special transitional grant (STG) money to sponsor private sector provision. The demand for respite services will undoubtedly increase as, with the closure of hospitals and hostels, more people live in the community with their families.

There were only two carers who did not use respite services but who expressed an interest in doing so. One person did not have a social worker and was trying to get one as a means of helping her to gain access to respite care. Most of the families not using respite care provision did not want to do so. Some felt they were coping satisfactorily without it and, because their learning-disabled relative could be left alone, the carers already had a degree of independence. However, a few family carers did not use respite services because they were unwilling to put their relative into the care of others, even when their caring responsibilities placed them under considerable physical and emotional strain. The carer cited below had experienced a poor service in the past and that experience, together with her daughter's poor health, made her unwilling to use respite services again. 'I don't mind looking after Sharon, I'm more worried when she's away than I am when she's at home... We'd be worried all the time. We haven't the trust in them, you see.'

Profile: Sue

Sue lives with her mum and dad and is one of the few people living with the family who did not go to a day centre. Several years ago, Sue fell out of the back of the day-centre minibus. As a consequence, her parents no longer trust the staff and believe the service to be under-resourced. The whole family is isolated because both parents are unemployed and they have no transport. Sue spends nearly all her time in a wheelchair. Her parents believe that sitting slumped in this position all day has led to repeated chest infections. The only formal support they receive is from a district nurse.

Those who did use respite provision found it extremely helpful and for some it was a life-saver. Family carers often had to be persuaded by other users or professionals of the benefits of this provision but having been persuaded to do so, it often proved to be a turning point in their lives. It offered immediate benefits. Freed from the routines and constraints of caring, many just took the opportunity to rest. Others were able to take a holiday. Respite care gave families the space to spend more time with their other children, who they felt missed out on 'ordinary' family activities because of the demands of their learning-disabled relative.

Individual planning and assessment

If the life chances of people with learning difficulties living in the community are to be maximised, it is important that their needs, circumstances and service provision are monitored and reviewed. The Individual Programme Plan (IPP; sometimes now called IP, Individual Planning) is well established as the cornerstone of assessment and planning for people with learning difficulties in the North West and elsewhere. When originally introduced, its emphasis on positive development made a change for service users who had previously been dealt with in a more passive way. Planning for people with learning difficulties had previously taken place in a context of deficits and 'problem' behaviour, if it took place at all. Individual Planning sets out to focus on the positive attributes of people. The principle that the service user is placed at the centre of service planning gives the opportunity for effective service user involvement. It also gives service providers the opportunity to create a service environment based on individuality (Walker & Racino, 1993; Smull & Burke Harrison, 1992). An effective IPP system gives the opportunity for service users and those close to them to evaluate the network of care and support available and to make adjustments in line with future goals and plans. This kind of review needs to take place regularly to ensure that changing needs or changing service imperatives are taken fully into account.

The IPP process was similar for all groups across all districts. However, there were significant differences in their frequency between the survey groups. As **Table 2.2** overleaf shows, the ex-hospital group were more likely to have had a review or IPP in the recent past. Almost three-quarters (73.3%) had an IPP within the previous six months, compared to just over half of the community and family groups. It had been more than a year since five people in the community group (16.7%) had had an IPP and three had never had one. The situation was worst for those in the family group, with nearly a quarter (23.3%) having not had an IPP. In the case of the ex-hospital group only three had waited more than a year and only one person had not had an IPP at all.

There was also considerable variation across the different districts in the study. The proportion who had had an IPP or similar

Table 2.2 Time since last IPP by Group (%)

Date of last IPP	Ex-hospital	Community	Family
<6 months	73.3	56.7	53.3
>6 mths – <1yr	20.0	16.7	10.0
>1yr – <2yrs	3.3	6.7	6.7
2yrs+	1.7	10.0	6.7
Never	1.7	10.0	23.3
Total number	60.0	30.0	30.0

review in the previous six months varied from 47.8 to 87.5%, and for those who had not had one for more than two years between 4.2 and 21.8%. In all areas the ex-hospital group tended to fare best. In one authority, those living with their families tended not to have had recent IPPs, while in another the community group did not do so well.

Regular IPP or similar reviews are important to ensure that an individual's situation is constantly monitored and reviewed, but the system will only be worthwhile if the whole process is meaningful to the parties concerned. The failure of IPPs to effect any change in the lives of the service users, for example, has been identified as an issue for concern (Sutcliffe & Simons, 1993). According to the responses of care workers in this study, people in the ex-hospital group were more likely to have seen a positive outcome from an IPP (*Table 2.3*).

Reviewing the process

As service users tend to find IPPs a very abstract experience, one of the local authorities in the study is currently reviewing its IPP process to find ways of making it a more relevant experience for all service users, including those with verbal communication difficulties. The importance of finding ways of making the process less bureaucratic (see Sutcliffe & Simons, 1993) and more meaningful to people with learning difficulties was illustrated by one of our respondents: 'Yeh, we have like paper, you know, we talk and Alice [key worker] writes down. I had that a while ago, you know, and Alice writes down. We talk and write down, you know, what would you like to do, you know. They ask me.'

Many people with learning difficulties in the study described their IPP as 'all right', some did

Table 2.3 Outcome of IPPs for Those Living in Formal Settings (%)

	Successful Outcome	Unsuccessful Outcome	Nothing Done	Don't Know
Ex-hospital	73.3 (n=45)	1.7 (n=1)	5.1 (n=3)	16.9 (n=10)
Community	46.1 (n=12)	15.4 (n=4)	23.0 (n=6)	15.4 (n=4)

not have much to say about the process at all. However, their comments showed that many did value the opportunity for involvement in the process, a finding which underlines the potential of an IPP system for effective service user involvement.

> 'Oh I think they are very good. Oh yes, they ask you what you're asking me now, you know: "Am I satisfied?" "Am I happy?"'

> 'They try and hear it from both sides, but I'm being asked, you know, what do I think? It's not just me sitting there listening to them, it's a two-way thing.'

However, there were also examples of professionals making key decisions about future planning at IPPs. One man who was asked who he thought was the most important person at his IPP replied: 'It's your key worker, because he decides what you do.' Another man said he felt the most important person at his IPP was his brother. Some service users, particularly those from the family group, reported that they did not attend all of their IPPs.

Some people with learning difficulties, living in formal care, complained that the IPP system did not lead to any change: 'Well to me it's all talk and do nothing. But I would like to have a meeting, a big one, to see what's going to happen in the future.'

The major criticism of family carers was also that IPPs did not make any difference. When one carer was asked if IPPs changed matters, she replied: 'No, not a lot really. You know, it just wavers a little bit here and there, but there's not a lot of change in it at all, no.'
'I don't think they are very helpful to be quite honest. No, it's to do with "pie in the sky". I think perhaps over the years I've become a bit cynical about these things.... You spend ages doing all these things and then it goes into a bloody great file that nobody ever opens again.'

On the positive side, family carers felt that the IPP process gave them an opportunity to share information with day centre staff and other service professionals. There is an obvious need for two-way communication between informal carers and service providers but the main purpose of the IPP process is to put the needs of the person with learning difficulties at the centre. In some cases this essential role as a forum for sharing information, experience and expertise to assist future planning appears to have been lost. Informal carers complained that the IPP process was not rigorous enough and, in particular, that the typical model of a one-hour meeting held once a year was insufficient for full consideration of all the issues involved. The issues of the regularity, length and pace of meetings must be addressed if there is to be any genuine attempt to involve service users in any meaningful way.

The more positive view of IPPs by formal care workers, particularly those working with people resettled from hospital, over family carers related to their relationship to the service deliverer. For most of those in formal supported settings, the individual responsible for setting goal plans was the person with learning difficulties' key worker. As well as being familiar with the needs of the service user, the care worker is also likely to take into account available resources when setting goals. The higher level of congruity between goals and outcomes — as defined by the care workers — is therefore unsurprising. The situation for family carers is of course different. Not only is their knowledge of overall service availability likely to be less informed, but they are also in a different relationship to service providers and purchasers. As a consequence, family carers said that though they did feel involved in the IPP meeting itself, their ideas and plans were ignored when things needed to be changed.

Needs of family carers

Another problem for family carers revealed by this study is that their own needs may not coincide with those of their learning-disabled relatives. For example, there is the case discussed in **Chapter Four** of the mother who refused supported housing for her daughter because she wanted her company and now needed her help to manage. There is of course much common ground but there are also tensions. In such circumstances who is the service user? Whose needs are being met? For example, day-centre care has a dual function (Flynn, 1994): providing people with learning difficulties with the opportunity to undertake activities away from home and providing much needed respite for hard pressed family carers. This can lead to a conflict between the need for the maximum number of sessions and the search for the best possible quality service. Where there is a conflict of interest between carers and the people they are caring for, this must be addressed with considerable sensitivity, which reflects both the very great sacrifices the carers have made and the ways their lives have been restricted by their caring responsibilities (Todd, Shearn & Felce, 1994), and the rights of the learning-disabled relative.

Conclusion

The research has revealed that there are considerable differences in the type and level of formal support provided to the different groups of people with learning difficulties living in the community. Those in formal care very often have a live-in care worker, or if they live alone a key worker who visits them regularly. However, they are unlikely to benefit from any other community services for people with learning difficulties such as day centre places, domiciliary services or respite care. Care workers were reluctant to ask for additional help in case it reflected on the way they were doing their job. At management level, the provision of additional domiciliary help or day centre provision for this group was given low, if any, priority because it would count as double provision on top of the permanent residential support. Furthermore such 'doubling up' could reveal inter-agency rivalry if, for example, the main caring authority, 'health', requested additional services from the social-services sector.

The situation for people with their families is quite different. Only a minority had any regular contact with a key worker. Very few had any formal sector help within the home. However, most had a day centre place and access to respite care, if not as often or as flexibly as they would like. The significance and implications of this finding are discussed at greater length in **Chapter Five**.

The pattern of care for the people resettled from hospital, with funding, was generally very similar to that provided to those who had been resettled within the community. However, there were some important differences, especially with regard to service reviews. There were much more significant differences in the pattern of care between all those in formal care and those with informal care. The goal of an integrated service for all set out in the *Model District Service* is clearly not being met. In the next chapter we consider the implications of the different types of care package given to the three groups with regard to service outcomes and quality of life.

Chapter Three
Living in the Community

One of the key functions of service provision for people with learning difficulties in recent times has been to enable people to develop competencies. Competence is identified as one of the lynchpins to both integration and valued social roles embodied in the theory of normalisation, as interpreted both by Wolfensberger (1972) and O'Brien (1985). For Wolfensberger in particular, the establishment of valued social roles is dependent on the enhancement of competence (Wolfensberger, 1972). The tendency for support services to over-indulge such an approach and put too much emphasis on training has led to some criticism, but it is important that services do not 'throw the baby out with the bath water'. Experience of other priority services, such as services for older people, has shown that where the emphasis is almost entirely on **care** for people rather than **support** for them to help themselves, the service itself creates dependency. It is essential that people with learning difficulties are given the opportunity to develop their competencies in order to maximise autonomy. Depending on the abilities of the individual, assistance might be given with personal care skills, undertaking domestic tasks, or social skills. In some cases, individuals may not wish to take advantage of the opportunities offered and this is their right. However, care and support workers should provide as much encouragement as possible to overcome the inertia or lack of confidence which may make a person reluctant to accept new challenges because in the past the care system has fostered their dependence on others.

There were some major differences between the sample groups in the level and type of competence training being provided. Over half of the community group (53.3%, n=16) were said to be receiving no competence or skills training, either formal or informal, compared to only a quarter of the ex-hospital group (23.3%, n=14). Just over one-quarter of the ex-hospital group (28.3%, n=17) and just under one-quarter of the community group (23.3%, n=7) had received and were also currently getting support from staff to enable them to develop skills in important areas of their lives.

The two staff groups also had different attitudes towards their role in carrying out skills training: two-thirds of staff working with the ex-hospital group said that they thought it was a very important part of their job; this was the case for only one-third of those working with the community group. Some of the reasons for care workers not endeavouring to encourage service users to develop new skills were related to age and are dealt with in the next chapter. However, others said that service users simply did not want to become involved:

'We've had a lot of changes in staff. We do occasionally get her to do things, but she isn't really interested.'

'We've done all we can with James, we've put a lot into him. Perhaps we've ignored the other two.'

'He needs to concentrate more, he always finds a reason not to do it.'

On other occasions staff did not see the need to teach skills, even though there might be some scope to do so: 'He is very good at most things that he needs to do. We're here to cook for him.'

Families are often portrayed as being reluctant to let their learning-disabled relative learn new skills because there is often an element of risk involved. However, we found a more varied picture. There were many instances of family carers trying to help service users to develop competencies in important areas and, among these, there was a certain amount of exasperation about the lack of support they received from day services in these endeavours. This ties in with the later discussion of day centres about whether these services do provide service users with constructive and positive opportunities. 'Christopher is one for an easy life, if he can get an easy way out of anything he will do. Whereas I think the Centre could be a lot more beneficial to him. I think they could get a lot more out of their clients.'

There were also instances where family carers (like care workers) found it easier and quicker to do the job themselves rather than support the person while he or she did it for themselves: 'I'm the worst person she should be living with, really... Like doing the washing up, you think, "Well, by the time she's done it, I could have done it," you know what I mean? So I do it myself, but I really should make her do it.'

There were other examples where opportunities for the person with learning difficulties to exercise more independence had not been given because the family carer was unwilling to take a risk or because they underestimated the skills of their relative:

'I've never really took the chance of leaving her on her own. I don't know what she'd do. Just say I took the risk, I mean I'd be wondering what she were doing.'

'Like I go out sometimes and say, "Don't answer the phone and don't open the front door," and immediately I come home, she's saying, "Oh such and such has been on the phone for you." You know she doesn't take any notice!'

The extent to which people with learning difficulties should be subjected to perpetual 'training' is difficult. A balance must be struck between the need to develop competencies, in order to widen the horizons of people who have often been over-protected by a care system which has put them in a situation of enforced dependence, and giving the individual the right, like anyone else, to sit back and say 'this is the way I want to live my life'.

Participation and presence or isolation?

Other research has concluded that living in an ordinary setting in a community does not guarantee success in terms of establishing social networks (Jahoda *et al.*, 1990) or using community resources and participating in community activities (Walker *et al.*, 1993). This study set out to look in detail at various indicators of participation and presence, that is, how far people were able to take part in activities outside the home and the nature of those activities.

We found that a significant number of people had not left the house in the previous week but that this varied by group. While nearly all of the people in the ex-hospital group had been out during this period, one-fifth of the community group and nearly one-quarter of the family group had not managed to go out for a week.

People in the ex-hospital group were most likely to have been out every day while only one in ten of those living with their family had managed to go out this often (*Table 3.1*).

Tables 3.1, *3.2* and *3.3* show that those in formally-supported settings, and particularly those in the ex-hospital group, had used a higher number and a more diverse range of community facilities in the four weeks prior to the interview.

Although those in formal care were able to get out and about more than people living with their family, many were not able to get out as much as they wanted. Even in the ex-hospital group, participation in outside activities was restricted. Care workers of people in the ex-hospital and community groups reported that over two-fifths (41%, n=37) were not able to go

out as much as they would like, all but four (89.2%) because there was not adequate staffing.

Outside activities are restricted because care workers based in shared accommodation have to balance the diverse needs of different people and inevitably basic care-needs take precedence over social needs (Walker *et al.*, 1993). Taking residents out can only be done when all practical personal care and domestic tasks have been completed. One man, aged 71, was now reliant on a wheelchair and could not go out unaccompanied. He enjoyed going to the pub but could not go as often as he would like: 'If the staff have got the time, you know, because I mean they haven't always got the time. They've got to do other things in the house, but if they've got the time they'll say "Come on".'

Table 3.1   Number of Times Person has Gone Out in the Past Week (%)

Number	Ex-hospital	Community	Family
None	3.3	20.0	23.3
1–3	26.9	26.0	56.7
4–6	31.7	26.7	10.0
7+	38.4	26.7	10.0
Total number	60.0	30.0	30.0

Table 3.2   Number of of Local Facilities Used in the Previous Month (%)

Number	Ex-hospital	Community	Family
2–5	20.0	53.3	46.7
6–10	36.7	16.7	53.3
11+	43.3	30.0	0.0
Total number	60.0	30.0	30.0

Table 3.3 Use of Community Facilities and Activities in Month Prior to Interview (%)

Place Visited	Ex-hospital	Community	Family
Hairdresser	88.3	63.3	70.0
Overnight stay	21.7	30.0	56.7
Shops	93.3	90.0	70.0
Bank/PO	88.3	70.0	36.7
Cinema	45.0	20.0	13.0
Theatre	20.0	26.7	16.7
Restaurant	93.3	76.7	50.0
Pub	85.0	66.7	53.3
Place of worship	28.3	10.0	20.0
Sport-spectator	31.7	10.0	6.7
Sport-participant	28.3	10.0	23.3
Social club	31.7	56.7	43.3
Library	20.0	16.7	10.0

Evenings and weekends

The clash between the social needs of people with learning difficulties and the availability of staff is particularly obvious during the evenings and weekends, when both parties want to be able to enjoy a social life. One service user who had been resettled nearly four years ago missed having an active social life outside the home: 'Oh, I watch television, you know, I just watch television and go on me bed, have a sleep on me bed, you know. Oh, I'd like to go for a meal, you know, and pictures and that, and in the pub, pubs, you know. I'd like to go out to a disco, yeah. I like to go out at night time, I don't think it's fair keeping us in at night time. We will when we get more staff though, we'll be going out.'

Going out is particularly difficult for people with mobility problems, but in some respects the practical issues involved are more easily overcome than their social isolation and lack of activities outside the home. Alan was resettled from Calderstones, a shared house with 24-hour support four years ago. He uses a wheelchair and, although going out is sometimes restricted by lack of staffing, he does get out some days of the week. He also has access to a car. His care worker described his typical day thus:
'[He]… gets his own breakfast with staff help, [helps with] domestic chores, collects his benefits, goes for a walk or drive, helps prepare tea. Shopping, watch TV and relax.'

Although people living in formal care tend to go out more often than people living with their families, the description of typical daily activities reveals a picture of relatively limited and sheltered lifestyles, which are focused around the home and domestic activity. Below are some examples of how the people with learning difficulties had spent the previous day, as described by the care worker:

> 'We went to the park, I [care worker] went to meet her. We looked through a few shops and came home. We had tea and went out to the pub.'

> 'Got up, bath, waited until others were ready. We did housework, went to do… shopping. Had a drink. Listened to personal stereo.'

> 'Household chores, makes his breakfast. Out and about, up and down the street. He came in and helped prepare tea. Watched TV, bath and bed.'

> 'She got up late — she's been getting up later, which I don't like. Went to the launderette, made her bed and did a bit of shopping. She had her lunch out and went round the shops.'

> 'It was her birthday so she opened all her cards and presents. She sat out in the garden for a while. We went to Manchester for lunch. In the afternoon she came home for a bit of a party.'

Care workers were also asked to describe how the previous weekend had been spent. Several said they did not know as they were not on duty — perhaps a little surprising. Weekends were opportunities, too, for some people to visit or receive visits from friends or family, for others the weekend differed little from weekdays. In some houses, there were more staff on duty at the weekend, which meant people were more likely to be able to go out. But in those where staffing levels were reduced

at weekends then, of course, opportunities for excursions were fewer.

> '[Sunday] He went to a car boot sale, went to watch local football, came home. He helped prepare tea and in the evening went to the pub.'

> '[Saturday] He got up and did the housework, went to Safeway doing the shopping. He prepared lunch. He went on a train to Halifax and went to a cafe. Back home and again cooked tea. In the evening, watched TV.'

> 'Saturday — nothing really because the other two had relatives round.'

> "Sunday — went out for the day and had lunch.'

> "The same as in the week — TV and that.'

Focus outside the home

In general, the descriptions of daily activities show how many of the people with learning difficulties in our study did become involved in everyday domestic activities. They may seem boring and humdrum but they are an essential part of everyday, ordinary living. What was missing, clearly, was any central focus *outside* the home. The majority of people had no regular commitments outside which could provide an external structure in the day. This, of course, is in certain respects no different to the experience of most people who are unemployed, but in this case there were staff working with some of the people with learning difficulties whose job it was to help them achieve integration in the local community.

People living with their families were the most restricted with respect to doing things outside the home. This finding is not surprising, given that family carers often had sole responsibility for their relative and were limited in the extent to which they themselves could get out and about. It also reflects the fact that people with learning difficulties living at home get little or no domiciliary support which could be used, for example, to take them out and many lack the resources to buy the help they need. None of the family carers used the sessional worker scheme, which was sometimes used to supplement the support given by formal carers. Not only did people living with their family have the lowest level of activity, but they were also much more dependent on special, segregated activities, such as social clubs for people with learning difficulties, which provide a ready-made social activity, with supervision. Their use of respite care accounts for the higher proportion of people in the family group who had had overnight stays away from home.

The social isolation experienced by disabled people living with their families has been highlighted elsewhere (Morris, 1993). As the two examples cited below show, family carers we spoke to were aware of the problem, but were sometimes powerless to do anything about it and sometimes indicated that they were not able to give community activities a high priority. This illustrates the importance of not judging informal care according to prescriptions and standards established in formal organisations and raises the more delicate questions of how to respond to informal care which tends to reinforce dependence and how the needs of carers and their learning-disabled relative can sometimes conflict. It also illustrates the need for families to receive more advice and practical support to encourage and enable them to extend the range of opportunities open to their learning-disabled relative.

Profile: Helen

Helen's father died five years ago. She now lives alone with her mother who is 82. She has no social activities of her own in the evenings and no transport to get to any outside events. Like most of the people living with their families, Helen has never had an independent social life but has only shared activities and contacts with her parents. Her mother said: '[She goes to the] day centre during the day. In the evening, well, she comes home and tells me what she's done. Then we have tea and then she washes up. By the time she's finished in the bathroom, we watch telly and go to bed at about ten o'clock. We never go out.

'I think she's isolated and I think we're inclined to get in a bit of a rut. But there again, I've got my housework to do, I mean I'm not paid just to look after Helen, I've got my shopping to do and all the other things that involve the home.'

Profile: Judy

Judy Hirst's life is a little more varied. She lives with her mother, father and brother. Although she keeps in touch with some of her old school friends, her main social network revolves around her family. When not at the day centre, she spends most but not all of her time in the house: 'We don't take her very far. We sometimes take her to functions at the social club: she's going out with us tomorrow night because there is a football presentation on... She watches telly — she's got her own telly upstairs and her own video... She sometimes goes to the cinema with a girl that she knew at school but that's very rare — so that's about it.'

Friends and contacts in the wider community

The extent of social networks and friendships is an important indicator of community participation. There is a tendency for care workers and others to present general acquaintances, such as with shopkeepers and people in the local pub, as friends. In this research, we were concerned to distinguish between these kind of general, though perhaps regular, contacts in the community from real friendships which have an element of reciprocity and intimacy. Nonetheless, it must be recognised that any social contact, particularly where the response is kind and friendly, can be an extremely important event in an individual's life.

One person who had moved out of a hostel said that the move had enabled him to re-acquaint himself with previous social networks. 'I went in [to the pub] New Year's Eve. I went with Sean that works here. Not seen people for years you know — for 20-odd years, more, and as soon as we walked in like, you know, people that I know, me mates, you know…Mmm, there were people comin' up to us: "What you havin?".'

The man quoted above had not seen any of the people he had met on New Year's Eve since then and was not likely to, as they did not know where he lived. This very positive encounter was obviously a significant event in his life, but clearly is not a long-term relationship based on loyalty and reciprocity. It is unlikely that meeting this man remained one of the major social occasions in the lives of those who greeted him so warmly in the pub as it had been for him.

There were considerable differences in the social networks of the three groups. The people who lived with their families tended to have the least outside contact (see *Table 3.4*) and what friends they did have tended to be primarily friends of their family carer. A significant proportion in each group — over two-fifths in the community group, over one-half in the ex-hospital group and nearly two-thirds in the family group — were said to have no friends at all of their own. Only one person in the ex-hospital group, only three in the community group and no-one in the family group had more than two friends. These are extremely worrying findings, especially as most of those in formal care had been in their

Table 3.4 Number of Close Friends by Group (%)

	Ex-hospital	Community	Family
None	51.7	43.3	63.3
1	26.7	20.0	33.3
2	18.3	26.7	3.3
3	–	10.0	–
4+	3.3	–	–
Total number	60.0	30.0	30.0

current setting for at least three years, and those living with their families usually much longer and perhaps most of their lives.

Chappell (1994) has identified a number of practical constraints which inhibit people with learning difficulties from making friends: the lack of autonomy in their everyday living; lack of and restricted access to money; and lack of staffing or staffing policies which inhibit opportunities for going out alone, especially in the evenings and weekends, and meeting people. While the first two constraints were applicable to the people in our study, we found that the last — the support necessary to enable people to go out — had the greatest impact. Without that support, the consequences of lack of autonomy for social isolation cannot be addressed. Also, while everyone in our study was dependent on social security benefits, which is itself a major indicator of poverty (Oppenheim, 1993), lack of money was rarely raised as an issue in any of our interviews because, we believe, the people concerned lived such restricted lives that this was not regarded as the most significant barrier to participation. This applied both to people living with their family and to those in formal care.

Living with the family and making friends

The level of support available is an important factor which influences people's ability first to make and then to sustain friendships, and participation in local activities is an important determinant of the opportunities open to people with learning difficulties to meet people and make friends (Garvey & Stenfert Kroese, 1991). However, as indicated above, those living with their families spent most of their leisure time within the home because they were dependent on unpaid volunteer help or on the principal carer's time and

energy level, to take part in leisure and social activities which were independent of those of their family carer. As a consequence, most of their social contacts were shared with the principal carer:

> 'She doesn't go out unless she goes with me.'

> 'She hasn't a friend of her own age, she goes out with us or she stays at home. I mean we obviously want to go out as a couple sometimes, so she stays at home and watches the telly.'

When a meaningful friendship did exist, contact was restricted to the day centre or other form of day provision. There was little evidence to suggest that people were able to meet friends outside the formal care setting. Some care workers argued that family carers were often not aware of any special friendships at a day centre, a symptom perhaps of the lack of involvement of family members in the day to day life of their learning-disabled relative outside the home, which is so important to maintain continuity.

The difficulty of making personal friendships, independent of the carers, was recognised on both sides as the following two quotes show: the first from a carer, the second from a service user.

> 'Not in particular, no. I mean he's friendly with everybody but no, I wouldn't say he's got one special friend because… I mean, he can't go out socially on his own. You're always there with him, you've got to take him, stop with him, bring him back.'

> 'Yeah, I have friends but they're family friends and an older generation. Any of my own age round about — I can't think of anybody. They're all grandmothers and aunties and uncles…I'm sure there

must be some sort of organisation where
people in the same boat as myself,
where the social side, with not having
any friends of your own age, there must
be something, you know where I could
go that'd solve that.'

Family carers obviously faced practical barriers
in the task of creating better community links
for their learning-disabled relative. However,
several regarded their son's or daughter's
disability as the barrier to even the most
limited contact with other people in the same
community. For some, this reflected the lack
of any real sense of community which would
welcome their relative, and their own sense
of isolation:

'You don't find in this day and age,
I think times have changed, people
all live in their own little communities.
I don't think they're really interested in
what happens to us.'

'No... we have a young couple that live
down there but basically everybody's out
at work. And of course by the time Peter
comes home at half past four, and he's
not in a sense allowed to play out
because he's a danger to himself...So
really, he's isolated in that sense to the
back garden, to the home.'

For others, it reflected their own very deep
sense of personal responsibility and their
unwillingness to impose their 'burden' on
anyone else: 'Well, no, I mean, if we let him go
out... sort of if we gave him freedom, he would
do. He'd be knocking on everyone's door.'

Of course, it is not only the person with
learning difficulties who is isolated. Their
family carers are often equally excluded by the
restrictions which their caring responsibilities
impose:

'We're absolutely housebound, we don't
live a normal life. Our life is from nine
[a.m.] until four in the afternoon... You
have to look and say that this is for the
rest of my life.'

'It's just that you can't go out. We couldn't
leave him. You know, you can't just up
and do anything.'

'You're sat there in the lounge babysitting
a 30-year-old daughter and thinking, this
is my life now, my God...At one time they
[friends] would ring up and say, "Look,
we're having this, do you want to come?"
We can't do it because we have got to
have someone here for Mary.'

There were four examples in the family group
of the person with learning difficulties having
a relatively large independent network of
friends. These highlighted the importance of
people being given the opportunity to access
existing networks, for example in sport, drama
or local politics, and the importance of finding
ways of enabling such participation for those
living in a family setting. Although all four
people had originally been introduced to the
activity and the network through their family
carer, all, like Ian, now had sustained networks
of their own.

Profile: Ian

Ian is 23 years old and lives in a small
village on the outskirts of Blackburn. He is
well known to all the people who live in the
village and well liked. One of the reasons
for Ian's large network of social contacts is
undoubtedly the role he has as assistant
greenkeeper and team member of the local
golf club. Both his parents and his grand-
parents are established members, which
is why Ian initially came to be involved.
However, since this initial introduction he
himself has become very accomplished at

the game and would not miss it, particularly when team events take place. These have brought Ian into contact with people from further afield in neighbouring towns and villages. In addition to taking part in events at weekends, Ian has the task of helping his father to prepare the greens and fairways as well as to help with the numerous social events on the calendar.

Formal care and friendships

If people with learning difficulties are to maximise the opportunities to form social networks and make friends outside the home, they will need the tacit and often the practical support of a third party. Enabling people to go out, take part in activities and meet new people should therefore be an important part of a care or support worker's job. In theory, the possibilities for making friends were more favourable for the people living in formal care settings. Most were living in small-scale shared accommodation with staff support, and the potential for making contacts both inside and outside the domestic situation was therefore better than for people living alone with their family carer and with no formal domiciliary support.

Our findings show that people with learning difficulties in the two formal care groups enjoyed a greater degree of community participation than the family-based group, which in turn put them in contact with people in the local community on a regular basis. As *Table 3.5* shows, unlike family carers, the majority of care workers believed that it was important for them to support the learning disabled person living in the community to build up a social network. However, the care workers of the ex-hospital group were more likely to regard it as important or very important, while few gave it very low priority. More care workers in the community group (nearly one-quarter) thought that this aspect of work was of little importance. In such cases. each individual was left to do what he or she could on their own, despite the fact that many of the service users in this group, even if they had the opportunities, lacked the necessary social and interpersonal skills to make friends independently (Bayley, 1994; Richardson & Ritchie, 1990; Brown, 1994).

Even when they were willing, the extent to which staff were able to help people develop friendships in practice was often constrained by pressures on their time. Just over two-fifths

Table 3.5 Importance of Helping Service Users to Develop Social Networks (%), as ranked by care workers

Care workers of:	Not important 1	2	3	Very important 4	5	Don't Know
Ex-hospital group	3.3 (n=2)	5.0 (n=3)	16.7 (n=10)	10.0 (n=6)	58.3 (n=35)	6.6 (n=4)
Community group	23.7 (n=7)	– –	23.2 (n=7)	26.7 (n=8)	26.7 (n=8)	– –

of the ex-hospital-group staff and just under two-fifths of the community-group staff said they did not have sufficient time to support people in this aspect of their lives. Over three-quarters of the care workers said that they had not undertaken any specific work in this area.

Living with others

People living in shared housing had opportunities to develop friendships with co-tenants or staff, though it is important to recognise that most often it was administrative convenience and resource implications, not friendship, that brought them together in the first place — only one-fifth of the ex-hospital group and one-eighth of the community group were said to have chosen their co-tenants. Although most people got on satisfactorily with the people they shared a home with, only one-third of both groups (31.1%, n=28) were said to have a specific friendship with someone else in the house. One quarter (23.3%, n= 21) of both groups were said to be living with someone they positively disliked.

The quality of relationship between sharers was rather more positive for those in the community group than for those in the ex-

hospital group (*Table 3.6*). Just over two-fifths of care workers of the ex-hospital group compared to nearly two-thirds of those working with the community group thought that the service user got on quite well or very well with the people they lived with. Two-fifths of the former were said to get on satisfactorily, but to have passive relationships, while 10% were said to get on badly. There is no clear evidence which might account for this difference. Booth and his colleagues (1990) found that the hostel workers they interviewed had more time to prepare residents for resettlement (partly because the hostel closure programme was delayed). Also, it is possible that, because hostel settings are smaller, it is easier to assess relationships than in the larger hospital and ward situation.

All shared living arrangements can give rise to problems like those described by one service user: 'We get on fine together. We can't help but fall out occasionally, but it's made up easily, you know. I mean Colin gets a bit moody sometimes, you know.'

For people with learning difficulties, incompatibility between people in the home setting has an extra significance because it

Table 3.6 **Views of Formal Carers on How People With Learning Difficulties Get on With the People They Live With (%)**

	Ex-hospital	Community
Very well	23.3	30.0
Well enough	20.0	33.3
OK/passive	40.0	16.7
Not well	3.3	3.3
Badly	10.3	0.0
Don't Know	3.1	17.7
Total number	60.0	30.0

can spill over into social and other activities outside the home, which are also often shared. For example, one man found that he was with a particular person he lived with, and disliked, at the day centre, too. When asked if he liked living where he did, he said: 'No, not much. I don't get on with Phil... I just don't like him. That's why I did a runner from [day centre]. I don't go there any more.'

The problem faced by many of those living in formal supported settings was that there was little alternative to the three- or four-person-group model. This particular kind of shared housing is experienced by non-disabled people for only short periods of their lives, usually when they are young and before they settle down permanently. Where shared accommodation is used, efforts must be made to enable individuals to influence the choice of those with whom they live and to offer opportunities for them to lead individual lives both inside and outside the home.

Only seven of the 90 people in formal care in the study lived on their own. There is a need for service providers to increase the choice people have in the kind of supported accommodation available. The reality, however, is that this model of care will continue to be popular with service providers, albeit possibly in slightly larger units which will exacerbate the disadvantages, as long as it is perceived to be the most cost effective. 'Financially if you have too many groups of two or less, we wouldn't have enough funding to run that... you have got to get the balance between the needs of the people and the funding' (Purchasing manager).

However, the cost argument is now being challenged. 'Supported living arrangements are generally no more expensive than group homes and congregate living. Often they cost less. Surprisingly, costs can be lower for people

with the greatest support needs. This is counter intuitive and challenges the traditional arguments about economies of scale... To illustrate: A person decided to invite someone without disabilities to live with her as a flat-mate. The flat-mate might live there rent free. Night staff are not needed which means a substantial saving in staff costs' (NWTDT, 1994, p15).

Keeping busy

One of the most consistent criticisms made of community provision for people with learning difficulties is the lack of regular and routine daytime activities. The problem stems, of course, from their almost non-existent participation in the labour market and, to that extent, this is a problem shared by other people similarly excluded: the unemployed, long-term sick and physically disabled and older people. People with learning difficulties face the added problems of being usually excluded for the whole of their life and of suffering considerable social stigma and therefore isolation. Their residual position in the workforce and the low expectations held of them by others are common experiences for all people with disabilities (Berthoud, Lakey & McKay, 1993; Walker, 1982). The major challenge then lies in promoting genuine employment opportunities for people with learning difficulties (Porterfield, 1988). A review of supported employment in the North West concludes that it offers 'a practical, attainable, *valued* option, and can compete with traditional day services in terms of quality and cost' (Ashton, 1995, p1). However, although 700 people are engaged in 40 schemes in the Region, demand exceeds supply and the most serious problem facing services is under-funding. The absence of work opportunities for the majority of people with learning difficulties is a huge barrier to their full integration in the community, as work is the means by which most adults maintain their identity. Work is also an important vehicle for expanding the individual's social network.

Paid employment

Only two people in the sample for our study were in ordinary paid employment. Both worked full-time. One, an ex-hospital resident, aged 47, was employed by the local authority as a road sweeper. The other lived with her family and was employed full-time working as a kitchen porter in a day centre for people with physical disabilities. One woman aged 44 served tea and coffee on a part-time basis at the WRVS. Four people, of whom three had moved from hospital, were employed in special employment schemes for people with learning difficulties: two of these worked in a garden centre and one worked in a small textile workshop; the fourth person in special employment lived at home and had recently started a work experience programme with an agency specialising in supporting people into ordinary employment. Two day centres had supported employment officers though no-one in our sample had benefited from this service. One person in the family group was using Training Into Employment, an Oldham-based

organisation which helps to support people with learning difficulties into suitable ordinary employment.

There were important differences in the use and access to structured day provision between the different groups (*Table 3.7*). Of the three, the family group was the one with the highest proportion of people having some form of structured day activity. All but four had some kind of provision. Similar proportions of the two groups in formal care had some structured day activities. However, these generally encouraging figures hide considerable diversity in the type and frequency of use of structured day activities and employment.

Education

Further education colleges were used by three out of ten of the people who had been resettled from hospital, but rather fewer of those who had moved from hostels or living with their families. Unfortunately, all too often people with learning difficulties attending college may find themselves within an integrated college but taking part in a segregated class. The segregation continues throughout the college day and people with

Table 3.7 Number of Sessions* Per Week in Structured Day Activities (%)

Number of Sessions	Ex-hospital	Community	Family
None	25.0	30.0	16.7
1 to 4	50.0	23.3	0.0
5 to 7	20.0	13.4	6.8
8 to 10	5.0	33.3	76.7
Total number	60.0	30.0	30.0

* including employment

learning difficulties find themselves using college canteens at times when other students are not present.

Day centres

The most common form of day care provision was provided in local authority day centres or Social Education Centres (SEC). Forty-five people (37.5%) in the sample went to a day centre. However, the frequency of use differed considerably between the groups, as shown in **Table 3.8**. People in formal care were much less likely to use day centres at all and, where they did, to do so for fewer sessions. By contrast, over three-quarters of people in the family group had access to them, the majority on a full-time basis.

The disparity between groups arises because people with learning difficulties living with their families tend to have been living in the locality longer but also because they tend to be given higher priority in the allocation of places (see **Chapter Two**). This is because they, and their family carers, get very little, if any, other formal service provision while those in formal care often have paid support within the home. One local authority was reluctant to offer places to people who had been resettled because the demographic trend locally showed that there

would be an increase in school leavers living with their families who would need day provision over the next three years.

Segregation or integration

There was also some reticence among service providers and care workers about people who had been resettled using segregated day centres, which was supported by the Regional policy of the integration of people with learning difficulties into general community facilities. 'In the past, separate arrangements for day activities for people who have been resettled from long-stay hospitals have often been developed by default…It is recommended that in the future the principle be adopted that equality of access to daytime and leisure activities be extended in each locality to all people with learning difficulties, irrespective of origin' (North West Region Review Working Group, 1989).

As a result, segregated provision was rejected in favour of the use of integrated activities with the rest of the community. Obviously, there is much to be said for this approach. With the correct levels of support, there is no reason why people with learning difficulties should not share wider, integrated community facilities. However, there are two problems.

Table 3.8 **Use of Day Centres (%)**

	Ex-hospital	Community	Family
0	77	67	30
1–2	7	7	–
3–4	10	7	3
5–6	7	10	0
7+	–	10	67
Total number	60	30	30

First, for reasons discussed elsewhere in this chapter, it is not always possible for people with learning difficulties even in formal care to fully utilise community facilities, or to do so on an equal basis with other users. These problems are particularly acute for family carers, who, as described earlier, often lack the time, money, physical strength or other personal resources to enable their learning-disabled relative to take part in a variety of community activities. Secondly, it has been argued that there is a role for some segregated provision which allows people with learning difficulties to operate in a non-stigmatising, non-threatening environment (Chappell, 1992). Also, if self-advocacy initiatives, based on group activities and mutual support, are to flourish, people with learning difficulties need to be able to meet together (Brown, 1994).

User involvement in choice of activity

In the past, day centre users have had little involvement in either the organisation of the centres or the choice of activities (Sutcliffe & Simons, 1993). The service users to whom we spoke were more often negative than positive in their attitudes to day centres and social education centres. In particular, several were critical of the cessation of the contract work which many centres had undertaken in the past and for which the workers received a token wage so as not to jeopardise their benefit entitlement. This change has been generally welcomed, particularly by the professionals involved. Unfortunately, although this change was made with the best of intentions by service providers, it was often carried out with only minimal consultation with service users and in many cases has not led to any new activities to replace those that have been scrapped.

'We used to do er…woodwork…We used to make bird tables… He stopped it…

We get bored, that's why I bring my tapestry…All these [others in the group], I'll tell you, and I'm not being funny, but all these are fed up.'

'Don't know, well I like it in a way but I get fed up with it. It's all the same things like, all the same things like passing the time away. Personally, I don't want that. I like to do things with me hands, like a job or something.'

'Oh not much really, that's why I think I get so depressed, there wasn't much to do really. They used to do movements to music and things like that. That's not my scene, silly things like that.'

Generally speaking, family carers spoke very highly of the day provision that existed. The exceptions to this were pointed out in the previous chapter and were associated with what some carers saw as a lack of motivation from day centre staff. But some carers did not know much about specific activities at day centres, the respite it gave them was regarded as being as much a part of the service as was the more positive role day provision could offer their learning-disabled relative.

Changes

In recent years, there have been important changes in some day centres, including some we visited in the North West, away from providing only centre-based activities to developing outreach activities in integrated settings (Carter, 1988). Some centres are now forging new links with other institutions and establishments open to all members of the community, for example, further education colleges. They then act as agents, organising access to courses for users and offering support when needed in the classroom. The centres themselves can promote community integration through the organisation of activities. One centre visited for the study offers flower-arranging classes with the local community college, where older centre users learn alongside other local people. However, changes in funding and management of further education colleges has placed such relationships in jeopardy. The success of outreach activities is also dependent on the availability of transport. If free transport is not laid on, those who cannot use public transport or who do not have access to private transport miss out.

As well as the organisation of outreach activities, the centres can provide other useful services. Staff within the day centre are often the only link family carers have with the statutory sector. They can provide a link between the family home, work or other placements. In such cases. they can play a central co-ordinating role for positive future planning, helping to put together well-structured, individually-planned activities for each individual. They could provide a similarly useful support function for formal care staff.

Some of the day centres we visited organised 'speak out' groups where development workers from local advocacy groups were invited in to help nurture advocacy skills. One centre used this service to facilitate meetings with service users in developing ideas on how to improve the services the centre offered. Elsewhere, service users were represented on interview panels. People living in formal care can benefit from a neutral forum in which they can voice their opinions and where they can learn from the experiences of people living in different situations. As a result of a 'consumers group' meeting in Manchester, one woman learnt about the other types of formal care settings available which enabled her to initiate a move from her current accommodation. Without meeting with other people with learning difficulties, she would have had neither the knowledge nor probably the confidence to initiate such a change.

With all its drawbacks, day centre provision provides people with learning difficulties, including those resettled from hospitals, with a separation between home and other activities. Care staff who worked with people who did not receive any day-time provision identified the fact that service users were completely reliant on the staff who supported them at home as being a major issue. Sometimes care workers argued that service users should have the opportunity to go off and do something with somebody who was not associated with their home support.

Money matters

Discussion of normalisation has tended to neglect the importance of money. The vast majority of people with learning difficulties rely wholly on the state benefits system for their income. Those few who have the opportunity to work are usually in low paid employment and may find themselves in a 'benefit trap' (Ashton, 1995, p1). There is considerable evidence to show that, in general, people living on social security benefits live in poverty and that social activities and entertainment are early casualties in the struggle to make ends meet on a low income (Walker, 1993). Davis and her colleagues (1993) illustrate clearly the various ways in which limited income restricts the lives of people with learning difficulties too — regardless of their living arrangements and yet, in practice, the care workers we interviewed seldom said that a person's opportunities for participation were limited by a lack of resources. The main reason for this is that people with learning difficulties are so excluded, (that is, take part in so few community activities) that they have few opportunities to spend their money and, therefore, to feel their poverty. Hence the main barrier to people in this study going out reported earlier was the lack of someone to accompany them, not lack of money.

People in formal care

As well as having extremely limited financial resources, many people with learning difficulties do not have, and never have had, any control over what money is theirs. Lack of money and lack of control over one's money are important constraints on an individual's autonomy. For people in formal care, money was deducted from the weekly benefits to pay for rent and weekly household expenses. The remaining money was then made available to the individual for personal spending. There was therefore no possibility, as with other people living on state benefits, of individuals falling behind with essential expenditures and getting into debt. In most cases (92.2%, n=83), care workers reported that service users had enough money to manage on.

There was some diversity in the degree of control each individual had over personal spending money (see **Table 3.9**). This could vary according to a number of factors: the individual's money skills, house practice and management rules. It is difficult to determine how much real say the people with learning difficulties in the study had over how their money was spent. The data shows that most of those who were thought able by their care workers to handle money were allowed to do so.

The control over his money given to one service user after resettlement from hospital was something he identified as a positive feature of his new life. As his carer said: '[He now has] confidence in handling his own money. He thinks it's marvellous for him to know it's his own money and he can spend it as he wants.'

There were only a few examples where people were not able to spend their money as they would wish. One woman was only allowed to buy a certain amount of cigarettes every day, in line with a goal set at her IPP. Staff in the local team office held the money of one man who lived independently, supported by a community team, because in the past he had spent his total weekly income in one day. He was given a fixed amount of money every day.

Care staff reported that there were numerous restrictions placed by line management on the use of service users' money. Nearly half (44%, n=40) said that approval had to be obtained for any expenditure over a certain limit, which in some cases — all of which concerned people who could not communicate verbally — had been refused. Some felt that this provided both the service user and member of staff with an important safeguard. However, others saw this as an unnecessary bureaucratic intrusion.

Table 3.9 **Amount of Say Over How Personal Spending Money Was Spent (%) For Those In Formal Care**

	Ex-hospital Group	Community Group
Independent	11.7	50.0
Some supervision	33.3	20.0
Very limited say	41.7	26.7
No say	13.8	3.3
Total number	60.0	30.0

Some examples of bad practice with respect to the use of people's money and their involvement in decision-making emerged in the research. In one instance, a member of the research team was present at the home of three women with complex disabilities when a table and chairs were delivered, much to the surprise of staff, let alone tenants. It was later revealed that the service managers were in the habit of ordering household goods and furniture, paid for by service users' money, without consultation with the people concerned.

People in family care

The financial situation of those people living with their family was not very different to those in formal care. All except one person were dependent entirely on state benefits. In most cases (83.3%) their money went straight into the general household kitty and personal spending money was given to them as they needed it. This finding is consistent with other research in the wider area of informal carers of disabled people and money management (Berthoud *et al.*, 1993; Grant, 1995). Not all of those in the family group who were given autonomy over their money were those whom a family carer said had no difficulty in handling money. Two of the five people in the family group who held on to their money after their benefits were cashed (although they did contribute to the household budget) were said to have difficulty in dealing with money. One woman was so concerned that she was not involved in how her money was spent, even though she admitted that she found money hard to cope with, that she had asked her local authority to find her a supported flat or house. For her, the lack of control she had over how her money was spent was symptomatic of other ways in which she felt her life was constrained. When asked why she would like to move out she said: 'Well, I could do what I want. I could go out when I want, stop in when I want and do things. Where I am now, I can't. My sister tells me what to do... My sister, she takes me money off me, even the money I get from here [day centre], she takes that off me.'

Financial hardship

Though the organisation of finances is similar for those in formal and informal care, in other respects their financial circumstances are very different. Previous studies of family carers have found that they suffer a double financial penalty — lower incomes and higher expenses (Qureshi & Walker, 1989; Glendinning, 1992). First, because of their caring responsibilities it is more difficult if not impossible for family carers to take paid work. Thus, over half (56.7%, n=17) of the families in the study were on benefit at the time of interview. Most of those who had retired had been unable to work because of their caring responsibilities when they were younger. Several regretted their inability to take paid work:

> 'If Steve didn't have a learning difficulty, I would work. I used to do school meals, but I found I was too tired in the evenings to cope with him.'

> 'I've never been able to take a full-time job because of Laura. I have to be here at 4pm and she doesn't leave the house until 9am, so it's impossible. I've always had to fit my life around hers.'

Some respondents reported that the benefits received did not fully meet the needs of their learning-disabled relative: 'You see, I had a statement made to me... she said that some people use part of the money [benefits] to subsidise their income. I'm afraid that is a fallacy because you are subsidising them!'

The second cause of financial hardship for family carers of people with disabilities stems from the additional costs which they often face (Martin & White, 1988). In this study, nearly half of the family carers said that they had extra *financial* costs because of the special needs of their learning-disabled relative. Transport, domestic equipment (such as frequent replacement of washing machines), special diets, heavy wear and tear on clothes and payment for respite care were all identified by unpaid carers as imposing an extra financial burden. Another common extra cost was the replacement of clothes due to incontinence.

> 'Possibly you try and buy food that is easy to cook, that makes it dearer.'

> 'Phone, food, cleaning, heating and because he is so clumsy he breaks things.'

> 'The washing machine and dryer get hammered because of his incontinence, we go through a lot of jeans.'

> 'Clothing, because she is incontinent and she ruins a lot of her clothes.'

Since the introduction of the *Social Security Act 1986*, there is little help available from the benefits system for this type of extra expense. Lump sum payments for occasional needs such as clothing were all but abolished in the Act and replaced instead by loans. As charging for services by local authorities becomes more common and more expensive, family carers and people with learning difficulties are likely to find their financial circumstances deteriorate further in the future.

Advocacy and empowerment

Leaving aside IPPs, there were very few examples of those living in formal settings having a role in how their lives and services were managed. Participation in planning services was practically non-existent for the people in the study. One exception is Bob Saville.

Profile: Bob Saville

Bob Saville is 73 years old and he lives in a house with two other men. The three were resettled from a hostel three years ago. The house is owned by a housing association and staffed by an independent provider. Bob is perhaps unique in that he has a place on the management committee of the organisation which staffs the house. He is the only service user representative on the committee. In addition, Bob is involved in the assessment of NVQs for the staff who work throughout the organisation. He has been involved at this level for over twelve months. He still feels a little nervous and at first admitted that he was just getting to know what was going on. But there was a significant attempt on behalf of the service managers to involve Bob who tried to make sure meetings were carried out at a pace he could cope with and to make information available before meetings. Bob still feels it is early days, but he is optimistic that his views will have an impact on the shape of the organisation.

Anecdotal information suggests that there were other people in the local authorities included in the study who were involved in planning at a local level, for example, one of the authorities has service user representatives on one of its planning committees. However, the study revealed that such opportunities for participation are rare.

An increasing level of attention has been paid in recent years to the importance of advocacy and self-advocacy as a means of giving service users a greater voice in all aspects of their life. Despite the fact that the North West has prided itself on providing user-centred services for people with learning difficulties over a number of years, we did not find any significant use of citizen advocates or self-advocacy groups, in this there has been little change since an earlier study (Walker *et al.*, 1993). Only a small minority of service users had access to citizen advocacy or paid volunteer schemes, all of whom lived in supported housing. No-one in the family group had this kind of support.

Three service users in the study had citizen advocates. Staff supporting a fourth man who had been resettled were keen to develop links with the local citizen's-advocacy organisation as they believed that he would benefit from an independent advocate. However, the man's mother was opposed to this move. Staff working with the few who did have a citizen advocate reported that while it was an extremely useful service in principle, it was not working well in practice. For example, one woman had not seen her advocate for several months.

A further five service users had people who provided them with support in community and social activities. Four of these were provided through a social-services-organised scheme and were paid for on a sessional basis by the service user. Although their role was not specifically that of advocating on people's behalf, staff recognised the potential of them taking on this role.

Three people with learning difficulties in the study took part in or made use of self-advocacy schemes. Two were based at their day centre, one went to a local group which met in the Town Hall. Care workers reported positively about such schemes: 'But she has been going to a few classes, you know... It's a make-your-own-mind-up sort of thing and it does seem to show with her at home, because you can tell she was saying "I'm going to do

this". She doesn't go now but it has left her with a more determined way to do things.'

The development of self-advocacy skills and personal empowerment can be achieved outside of citizen advocacy and self-advocacy groups. Many care workers reported that the people they worked with, particularly those who had been resettled from hospitals, had become more independent and self-confident. Just over two-fifths (43.3%, n=26) of care workers of the ex-hospital group said that service users had developed skills in this area and seven (23.3%) of the community group were said to have made similar progress.

'A lot of work to be done. She now does things when she wants rather than be told. She will now advocate for herself, not always. She's a lot more capable with household tasks. She loves spending money on clothes.'

'Assertiveness, more capable of making choices, more choice in the house.'

'She makes more decisions, communication may come along. She learns skills very slowly.'

There had also been development of these skills for some of those living at home. Informal carers admitted that this was not always easy for them but it was something that they welcomed. The female carer quoted below had only recently contacted the social services department. Since then staff had been working with her daughter to identify what she wanted in terms of future housing and support. The parents had been persuaded to leave their daughter alone in the house for a week. This had an important spin-off for her self-confidence which is clear in the second quotation:

Mother: 'I'm not saying that she has never been naughty, or ever done anything wrong, we've had more sort of antagonistic behaviour since we started this programme, with this process than we ever had. She's started to think for herself and I wonder sometimes if in the past she has just gone along with everything. It's good to see because she's got a mind of her own.'

Daughter: 'I have had a spell, it were only for a week, but I have had a spell where I had the house, the responsibility and everything else for a week. And those few days were oh, you know, that week, oh, it really pointed me in the right direction.'

Conclusion

The data from the study of the three groups of people living in the community (those who have been resettled with funding from a long-stay hospital, those who have been resettled within the community from the family home or a hostel, and those who are living with the family) confirms that there are differences in the packages of care and support they receive and that this has direct implications for their quality of life. Generally speaking, these differences stem, not from the needs of the individual, but from their service background and depend on where, and with whom, they are living. Our findings confirm that there are differences in services provided for people living in the formal care sector according to whether they were resettled with a dowry or not. The former tended to have higher levels of staffing, to go out more, take part in more activities and have more friends. However, not all the differences can be attributed to resources. Staff working with the people who had moved out of hospital tended, for example, to be better trained and be more likely to stress the importance of helping people to go out and make friends.

While there was a gap in service provision for the two groups in the formal care sector, there was a much wider and significant gap between both these groups and people with learning difficulties living with their families. These people, and their family carers, received virtually no support outside of day centres and occasional respite care.

While there are obvious inequalities in both the level and type of services provided for people with learning difficulties according to their service origin, the implications for quality of life are a matter of degree. There are important similarities as well as differences. All three groups face serious disadvantages within their communities. While people living with their families are the most socially isolated, there is an acute lack of real employment opportunities, of flexible and varied leisure and educational activities outside the home, and limited opportunities to establish and maintain independent social networks for all the people with learning difficulties included in the study. The level of autonomy achieved by each individual was dependent on the extent to which either formal care workers or family carers were willing and able to relinquish control to the individual concerned. If the conditions were achieved by which people with learning difficulties could participate to a greater degree in community activities, with all the implications that has for personal expenditure (including the cost of activities, the cost of equipment or fashionable clothes to be seen in), then many more would find, like other groups of social security claimants, their lives restricted by the benefits on which nearly all depend.

Other research has shown that living in the community offers people with learning difficulties a far more positive and constructive quality of life than that provided by segregated, institutional care (Emerson & Hatton, 1994). The solution to the problems discussed in this chapter must be confronted within the community care system. There is an obvious need for integrated service provision, based on need rather than service origin. Although those resettled from hospital were found to have advantages over the other two groups, it is clear that improvements for the latter should not be made at the expense of the former. The lives of the ex-hospital group are already restricted by the levels of care and support available and any further dilution would make 'ordinary living' unworkable in any meaningful sense. Rather, the objectives of policy-makers and service providers should be to use the very positive experience of those who have been resettled and build on them to enhance the lives of all people with learning difficulties living in the community. Furthermore, if local services are to truly reflect and respond to service users, greater emphasis will have to be given to their participation at all levels of service planning and delivery, as suggested by the Social Services Inspectorate (SSI, 1994). This will entail the establishment of effective systems and procedures involving people with learning difficulties, and a re-evaluation of the process of participation, away from traditional planning procedures which allow only for token representation rather than genuine participation as an equal partner.

Chapter Four
Older People with Learning Difficulties

One of the great social achievements of the twentieth century has been increased longevity. Advances in medical care and social support for people with learning difficulties means that this group is also living longer. In the past, the ageing of people with learning difficulties was both partial and hidden. On the one hand, those with severe learning difficulties had relatively short life spans and, on the other, many of those who survived into late adulthood were likely to be invisible, either in institutions or in the often protective care of their families. The concepts of learning disabilities and learning difficulties were applied exclusively to childhood (Farnham-Diggory, 1978). Moreover, when the issue of ageing among people with learning difficulties was first raised, the concern was not with gerontology but with adult development in middle age (Dybwad, 1962).

Until recently, the issue of ageing among people with learning difficulties received relatively little attention in Britain, either by the academic community, with the notable exception of Hogg and his colleagues (Hogg *et al.*, 1988), or policy makers. Social scientists have recognised the high incidence of disability in old age (Townsend, 1981; Martin *et al.*, 1988) and, more recently, have looked at the experience of those with physical disabilities as they get older (Zarb, 1991; Zarb & Oliver, 1993) but research on people with learning difficulties, particularly the recent series of studies of hospital closure and relocation, has

not discussed the ageing dimension (see, for example, Booth *et al.*, 1990; Korman & Glennerster, 1990).

A number of issues arise when considering health and social care provision for older people with learning difficulties. First, given the fragmentation of service provision, who holds primary responsibility for their support: learning difficulty services or those for older people? The very different traditions and models of care provided by the two sectors can have a crucial impact on the type of service provided. Related to this is the question of how appropriate the concept of 'normalisation' is for older people with learning difficulties, because mainstream 'normal' service provision and, indeed, the lifestyle of many older people, is constrained and stereotyped. Second, for those living with their families, there is the question of how far the needs of the informal carer coincide or conflict with those of their relative who has a learning difficulty, and whose needs service providers are trying to meet in practice.

One of the aims of this research was to look at the circumstances of older people with learning difficulties to see how far age was a factor in the attitudes and services which they experienced, as well as to see how far both learning disability services and services for older people were responding to this new user group.

The following discussion concerning the quality of life and provision for older people with learning difficulties must be set within the context of the profile of the older people included in the study, which is set out in **Appendix Two**. This shows that, while more older people did have a physical disability or long-standing illness, they were likely to have lower levels of learning difficulty than those in the younger group. This difference has mainly come about because the chances of babies with severe learning difficulties surviving have improved with each generation; babies with very severe learning difficulties born over 50 years ago would have had much less chance of surviving into adulthood than their contemporary counterparts. Also, 50 years ago it was not uncommon for people to be committed to mental handicap institutions for social reasons, for example, because a single woman was pregnant. Such people are still found living in institutional care. As a consequence, older people with learning difficulties tend to be more able than younger generations, though of course many have been handicapped by years of institutionalisation. It is important that service providers and others acknowledge this important factor, because the stereotyping of older people as being too old or unwilling to learn may be even more inappropriate for those with learning difficulties than it is for the wider population.

Normalisation and older people

Today, the principles of normalisation have widespread, though not uncritical, acceptance (Brown & Smith, 1992; Chappell, 1992) and have had a considerable influence on the development of services for people with learning difficulties in both Europe and North America. The particular operational model of normalisation that has had greatest influence in the UK is the 'five accomplishments' (O'Brien, 1985) and, as noted previously, it is this model that was incorporated into the strategy of care for people with learning difficulties drawn up by the NWRHA.

The application of normalisation to service provision has been criticised for neglecting gender, class and race (Brown & Smith, 1992). The same criticism may be levelled with regard to age. Although normalisation theory hinges on the position of the individual, in making it operational through service delivery, attention is inevitably concentrated on group needs, interests and expectations and, if it is inappropriately applied, this can lead to stereotyping. Normalisation is concerned with what is socially valued. However, where the reference or peer group in the wider community, that is, older people in general, is itself not socially valued, and where the main models of care provided for the wider group neither aspire to nor achieve the core values of normalisation, then, unless challenged, the goals set for older people with learning difficulties will be constrained. This sort of dilemma is familiar to social gerontologists who have, for example, questioned the denial of poverty (Walker, 1980) or disability (Townsend, 1981) in old age on the grounds that these are 'normal' features of ageing. Our previous research found that care workers tended to treat older people with learning difficulties differently and to have different expectations of their abilities and appropriate lifestyle (Walker *et al.*, 1993). This has important implications for the nature of the support or care which is provided and, in particular, whether the care of older people with learning difficulties is structured on the expectation of dependence rather than the goal of increasing independence or, preferably, inter-dependence.

Independence versus dependence

If people with learning difficulties are to be enabled to develop independently, considerable attention must be given to their continuing training needs to ensure that they maintain skills which have been learnt and that they develop new skills and competencies. Previous research has found that older people with learning difficulties tended to receive much less skills training than their younger counterparts (Walker *et al.*, 1993). Only three-in-ten people aged 60 or over were currently receiving any training or had received any in the previous twelve months compared to eight out of ten of those under 60. This included informal domiciliary training as well as formal training courses. In 30% of cases, support workers of the 60-plus age group thought that training was not an important part of their job, while only 5.3% of those working with the 50–59 group and none working with the under-50s shared this view. They were also more cautious about older people's ability to learn. Only 18% of the older group who might have benefited from skills development were deemed capable of learning a new skill, compared to 33% of the younger age group. Such stereotyping, based on the popular misconception that 'you cannot teach an old dog new tricks', has been found in the labour market where employers believe, incorrectly, that older people are harder to train (Taylor & Walker, 1994). In fact, operational research shows that older workers just require different training methods to younger ones (Belbin, 1965; Belbin & Belbin, 1972; Warr, 1993).

It is not necessarily a bad thing that training is not provided. Indeed, some would argue that older people should be allowed to sit back and relax. Of course, we are not suggesting that training should be forced on people. However, it is important that each individual should be given the opportunity to fulfil their own potential as far as he or she would like. By making ageist assumptions, service providers can restrict the range of opportunities available to older people. In the past, few people with learning difficulties have had the opportunity to fully exploit their own potential, especially with relation to independent-living skills, because of the institutional and over-protective models of care that have been in operation. Older people, who have lost out most, have been proved capable of gaining greater control over their own lives if they are given the opportunities and skills to do so:

> 'His disabilities might handicap him as he gets older, but James should go from strength to strength. He's got more capabilities in him.'

> 'No matter what your age, if you need support, you need it.'

> 'The thing is we don't look on them as older people or disabled people, they are themselves.'

A second explanation for the reluctance of care workers to invest in skills-training for older people might be their assumption that this group would become less independent in the future (see ***Table 4.1***).

Only one-third of those working with the over-60s thought that they would become more independent in the future, while three-quarters of those working with the under-50s believed that this would be the case. By contrast, one in five thought that those over 60 would become less independent, while none of the care workers of the under-50 group thought this would happen. However, as the discussion of older people living with their families and reports from care workers show, older age does not necessarily bring greater dependency. Given the opportunities, older people with learning difficulties can develop

Table 4.1 Care Workers' Expectation of Future Independence of Service Users by Age (%)

	Under-50	50–59	60-plus
More	75.0	47.8	33.3
Same	20.0	39.1	44.4
Less	–	13.0	18.5
Don't Know	5.0	–	3.7
Total number	40.0	23.0	27.0

new skills and interests and adapt to new circumstances:

'He's got quality of life now. He's his own man and can please himself. Health-wise I think we do better. I think everything is better.

'I think they're treated as old people and in their minds they're not. I had them reading and writing but it's all gone by the way. The staff are very nice people but they're not helping to make Kenneth independent. He's safe and secure and he has somebody to look after him and he is occupied Monday to Friday…but you need more than that in life.'

The second remark was made by a social worker who had worked with Kenneth when he lived in a hostel and had assisted him when he moved out into sheltered accommodation, where there were other people with learning difficulties. She was contrasting the way she had supported him in the past with the care that he was receiving currently and the difference between the two approaches with regard to his independence.

Care workers reported that younger people were more likely to have become more competent and independent in recent years. However, in looking at other parts of the data,

which are discussed below, it is clear that the responses reflect not only their perceptions of the abilities of the person with learning difficulties, but equally importantly the lower expectations held of them by care workers and the more restricted opportunities they offered them.

'I feel that younger people should learn more, whereas older people may not need training.'

'There aren't so many options for older people. There are fewer activities for someone who is old and disabled.'

Although care workers said that double discrimination against older people with learning difficulties did not exist, in practice it clearly did. We frequently encountered statements made by those working with older people that, although well meaning, contained implicitly age-discriminatory assumptions. Some of these are illustrated below:

'Anthea's old key worker would say she shouldn't be set goals because she is too old. I don't agree. I think everybody should have the chance.'

'I'm hoping that he will become more independent but I'm worried that because of his age he may not.'

'[He's] growing old gracefully. [We] can't be so hard now, [he] can relax.'

'Easier with younger [people, they're] not as set in their ways.'

'Younger people need new things. They need to get out more. Older people are more content.'

The behaviour of care staff holding such assumptions may result in practices which reinforce dependency rather than creating empowerment. Contrary to the limited expectations of older people which were frequently expressed, our findings support previous research (Maaskant *et al.*, 1994) which shows that there is no inevitable relationship between age and dependency. Comparison of the data collected six months after resettlement with that collected as part of this study, some three years later, shows that the relationship between age and dependency is not as clear-cut as many care workers and policy-makers believe. (See *Table 4.2*.) Over this period, people in both the younger and older age groups gained in independence according to

a number of measures: approximately one-fifth of people over 50 had improved their skills in communication or personal care; over one-quarter were better able to use and understand money and were better able to exercise choice. In the majority of cases there had been no change in skill level. In a minority of cases there had been some deterioration but, in fact, this was greater within the younger group than in the older group.

Care workers reported that the younger group's behaviour had led to increased independence in a number of areas. The only respect in which older people were reported as having more independence was with regard to their participation in household activities. Younger people did better with regard to behavioural changes, social skills and their ability to self-advocate.

The slower progress made by older people might be age related but, equally, it could be an inevitable outcome of the limited opportunities that are made available and

Table 4.2 Increased Independence According to Skill, for All in Formal Care (%)*

	Under-50	50–59	60-plus
Personal care	11.3	11.1	–
Communication	1.6	7.4	–
Behaviour	12.9	–	6.5
Social skills	9.7	11.1	6.5
Self-advocacy	27.4	22.2	32.2
Household jobs	16.1	22.2	6.5
Mobility	9.7	–	9.7
Other	12.9	7.4	3.2
Total number	40.0	23.0	27.0

* Respondents could give more than one answer

the expectations of care staff. Younger people tended to be encouraged to speak out more for themselves and to do and act more independently.

'I'm hoping he will become more independent, but I'm worried that because of his age he may not.'

'I don't think we've got the staff [to enable her to become more independent] but her age is probably something that will hold her back.'

Keeping busy or passing the time?

As **Chapter Three** shows, most of the people with learning difficulties, and in particular those living in formal care, lacked regular structured activities outside the home. This is also a problem common to many older people after retirement. It is not surprising then that older people in our study were twice as likely as younger people to have *no* regular structured activity outside the home and overall to have fewer regular organised activities. (See **Table 4.3**.)

Even among the family group who did have greater access to the main day care provision, namely day centres, there was a major disparity by age. Only 9% of the under-50s

had no day provision, compared to 25% of the 50–59 group and 50% of the over-60s. The *type* of structured activities outside the home undertaken by respondents also varied according to age.

Day centres within the study did not operate any formal retirement policies and yet, as **Table 4.4** shows, there was what amounts to a tacit retirement policy in operation. People over 60 were much less likely to use day centres for people with learning difficulties and care workers themselves reported examples of age discrimination. '[I] don't think it's right that day centres won't take people over 65. The Age Concern one is a charity and doesn't have the same resources. It's not fair to turn round and say, "Happy 65th — you can't come here any more".'

While many existing users, especially those living with their families, were able to continue to attend day centres as they got older, new older users were unlikely to be given a place. In addition, this group had less favourable access to further education colleges — one respondent, for example, was refused a place because he was too old — and virtually no access to employment. A survey of supported employment in the North West found that 95% of those in work were under 50. Thirteen of

Table 4.3 **Number of Sessions of Structured Activities in One Week by Age: All Respondents**

No. of Activities	Under-50	50–59	60-plus
0	14.5	18.5	48.4
1–4	27.4	40.7	29.0
5–8	24.2	22.2	9.7
9+	33.9	18.5	12.9
Total number	62.0	27.0	31.0

the 40 schemes in operation did not support anyone over 50. The author concluded that: 'This is certainly well below the level expected in the non-disabled working population. It could be that, because of the very limited resources available generally, this group is not seen as a priority' (Ashton, 1995, p17).

This under-representation of older people with learning difficulties in supported-employment schemes reflects the growing marginalisation of people over 50 from the labour market which results from age discriminatory employment practices. As a consequence of such discrimination, the older people in the study had even fewer opportunities to take part in regular organised activity outside the home than younger people.

General services for older people might be expected to provide an extra avenue for outside activity for older people with learning difficulties. However, few older people had much contact with these services (see **Table 4.4**). As these services now tend to cater for

the very elderly, the 50–70-year-olds — a group which one care worker remarked was extremely poorly catered for — might have been deemed too young to be accepted. However, there is also a reluctance by the older person's service sector to take on people with learning difficulties. As a result, older people with learning difficulties fall between the two service sectors — a clear case of double jeopardy.

'I think they are a bit patronised... They are people with learning disabilities first rather than older people. Therefore, if you try to get them into an old people's service, the learning disability precludes them. Community care and day centres provided for the elderly don't cater for those with learning difficulties — they are expected to muck in.'

'She's too old to go to a day centre but at the over-60s club they don't want her because of her disability...Nothing there for them. You get the normal older people centres but they don't welcome

Table 4.4 Type of Structured Activity by Age: All Respondents (%)

No. of sessions	Under-50	50–59	60-plus
Employment	3.2	3.7	–
Special employment	4.8	–	3.2
Day-centre for people with learning difficulties	46.8	40.7	16.1
ATC	12.9	11.1	6.4
Outreach service	6.5	–	3.2
College	27.4	29.6	9.7
Older people's day centre	–	11.1	16.1
Other	19.3	22.2	12.9
Total number	53.0	27.0	16.0

people with learning difficulties…and the Gateway Clubs [clubs for people with learning difficulties], for instance, are not appropriate for older people.'

Three people in their sixties had experienced problems with other non-learning disabled people when using older people's services. One man, who lives in a sheltered housing complex for older people, was asked not to go on outings organised for tenants. Another woman who had a 'reputation' for her behaviour was asked to stop attending a lunch club. At other activities for older people organised by the Salvation Army she was finding it difficult to fit in:

> 'Well I go for my dinner to Salvation Army, but they want you to go to the service. And I go again on a Monday but I'm not keen on it there 'cause they don't want to know you. Monday afternoons and we have a game of bingo. They don't want to know you, you know how some people are, they just don't want to know you. The minister and one or two of them's all right.'

Care workers of younger people, who had less actual contact with services for older people with learning difficulties, had a generally more positive picture about the quantity and quality of service provision. This might well reflect the 'must be' syndrome, that is, there *must be* services because the need is so obvious.

This is an over-optimistic view which has been proved inaccurate in many areas of service provision. Over two-thirds of those working with people over 50 thought that the general level of services for older people with learning difficulties was poor or very poor and yet several reported the closure of appropriate facilities in the recent past.

Only 12 people over the age of 50 received older people services (three aged between 50 and 59, seven aged between 60 and 69 and two over 70). Seven people were in warden-controlled flats for older people. Five went to an older person's day centre. Most support workers thought that this provision was appropriate but four were not happy with it. A further four of those over 60, living in formal care, had been identified as needing some kind of older people day service but had, as yet, been unsuccessful in finding a placement. One woman who had been resettled from one of the large hospitals was turned down after assessment because she already had day care in the form of her home support workers. The lack of appropriate facilities was illustrated by the following care worker: 'When we are invited to events they are always geared towards younger people…I wouldn't say [services for older people] were very good. Everything just seems geared for younger people.'

When one service user was asked what she would want from older people's services, she stressed the need for external activities which gave some structure and difference to day-to-day living: 'Well, same as you say, if I could find 'em somewhere to go during the day, get out the house more. I mean, really, when you've been out the house, you feel a lot better for it… Otherwise you get grumpy and depressed.'

Although younger people had made slightly more use of community facilities in the previous month (**Table 4.5**) and were considerably more likely to have taken part in a greater number of activities (**Table 4.6**) in the previous week, care workers were more likely to say that people in the younger age group were restricted in their activities by lack of adequate support. Some 65% of the younger group were said to have been unable to do something they wanted because there was

Table 4.5 Number of Community Facilities Used in the Last Month, by age: for those in formal care (%)*

Number	Under-50	50–59	60-plus
0–4	7.5	21.7	18.5
5–7	47.5	26.1	55.6
8+	45.0	52.2	25.9
Number	40.0	23.0	27.0

Table 4.6 Number of Activities in the Last Week, By Age: For Those in Formal Care (%)*

Number	Under-50	50–59	60-plus
0	10.0	4.3	11.1
1–4	22.5	52.7	44.4
5–7	22.5	17.4	18.5
8+	45.0	26.1	25.9
Number	40.0	23.0	27.0

* Tables 4.5 and 4.6 do not include people living with their families. This group tended to use community facilities less but this did not seem to vary with age.

no support available, compared to only 46% of those over 60. While 7.5% of care workers of the under-50s and 32% working with the older group said that the person with learning difficulty could not undertake their favourite activity as often as they would like, most commonly because of staff shortages.

Care workers were more likely to report that older people preferred indoor activities, such as watching television, listening to music and knitting, while younger people were said to enjoy going out to the pub, restaurants, cinema and football matches. Only one-quarter of the younger group were said to most enjoy home-based activities compared to over half of the

older group. However, a similar proportion of the over-60s were reported as being able to go out alone and interviews with the service users themselves seemed to indicate that people of all ages enjoyed a mixture of activities, inside and outside the home:

'I like going to cricket if it's a nice day. I went on Sunday. We're going on holiday soon as well' (aged 65).

'Well, we were [going out], but not at the moment. We don't go out through the week, only if they've got enough staff to take me. The only day I go out is on a Sunday, when I go out with my friends' (aged 70).

'Well, I sometimes go to the pub, sometimes to the pub and for a walk, you know. I sometimes go to the cinema with my girlfriend' (aged 52).

Families and friends

Of those receiving formal care, all but three of the younger group (92.5%) and all but 11 of the over-50s (78%) were in touch with a family member (see *Table 4.7*). Of these, 84% of the former and 77% of the latter had seen them in the previous 12 months.

Unsurprisingly, a higher proportion of the younger group than their older counterparts were in touch with parents. However, a significant number of even the oldest people were still in touch with a relative. Three out of five of the people over 70 and four out of five of those aged 60 or over were in touch with someone. For the older group, the relative with whom the person was most frequently in touch was a sibling. Two-thirds of support workers reported that the relationship between the person with learning difficulty and their nearest relative was close. This did

not vary according to age or to the relative concerned. However, younger people tended to see their relatives more often: 57% of the under-50s with a relative saw their relative more than once a month, compared to only 37% of those over 50 who were still in touch with a family member.

As discussed in *Chapter Three*, a significant proportion of all those living in formal care had no friends outside the home (see *Table 4.8*), but this was slightly more likely in the over-50s: 52% versus 40% with one friend or more. The most common place for service users to meet new friends was at facilities for people with learning difficulties, two out of five friendships for people in both groups had been made in this way. However, the albeit limited use of facilities for older people meant that five older people had made non-learning disabled friends. Nobody under 50 had made a friend through the use of open community facilities. Other friendships had been made prior to the move into the community and were therefore usually also with learning disabled people or with neighbours.

Table 4.7 **Proportion of People with Close Contact With a Relative, By Age: In Formal Care (%)**

	Under 50	Over 50
Parent	47.5	10.0
Sibling	22.5	36.0
Aunt/Uncle	2.5	6.0
Other	7.5	16.0
Number	32.0	34.0

Table 4.8 Proportion of People with Friends Outside the Home, By Age: In Formal Care

Number of Friends	Under 50		Over 50	
	Number	Percentage	Number	Percentage
0	24	60	24	48
1	16	40	26	52
2	9	22.5	12	24
3	2	5	3	6
4	2	5	1	2
5+	2	5	–	–
Total number	55		66	

Growing older within the family

The nature and extent of formal support given to families caring for relatives with learning difficulties is discussed in **Chapters Two** and **Three**. There are, however, some issues which are specific to older people with learning difficulties and their carers. Eight of the people still living with their families were 50 or over and the oldest was 68. Four lived with a parent, one of whom was a foster parent, three lived with a sibling and one lived with her husband. The parents were aged 80, 82, 84 and 93. In the last case, the learning disabled daughter lived with her increasingly frail, and largely bedridden mother. They managed with the help of the former's brother and especially a sister who called in every day and who generally organised the household.

Several of the older people with learning difficulties had faced increased physical disability: two in particular had problems with their sight. One other person, whose learning difficulty had been minor most of his life had developed a phobia about cancer and now needed much more support. Nonetheless,

family carers did not display the ageist attitudes that were evident among some formal service providers. On the whole, the families were not concerned that their relative's capabilities would deteriorate due to age. One specifically thought that the reverse had happened and in some cases the service user was assuming greater responsibility in their older age. This is not to say that family carers did not see limitations in what their relative could do to gain greater independence, but rather that age was not regarded as the cause of those limitations. This is, we think, an important illustration of the differences in the social construction of old age that may sometimes exist between primary (informal) relationships and secondary (formal) ones: the former can operate successfully without a chronological definition of old age, whereas such definitions have become more and more important in formal relations, such as in the labour market, over the course of this century (Walker, 1980, 1982; Qureshi & Walker, 1989).

Changes in the relationship between carer and their learning-disabled relative tended to be related more to the age of the former than the latter. In two cases, the roles between the two had reversed and the daughters with learning difficulties concerned began to look after their mothers. One did everything in the house, from shopping to cooking hot meals and sorting out the bills. The other has more limited abilities but learnt to use a microwave with help and to telephone other family members if the need arose. In these instances, where the original carer needed to be cared for, the person with the learning difficulty had taken over the caring role and, in so doing, had developed more independent living skills.

This role reversal is one illustration of how the needs of the 'carer' and the person they are caring for can overlap and even conflict in the family situation. It is common for family carers not to want their learning-disabled relative to leave home. Often, this is because they are not confident of the quality of care which will be provided. However, in some cases, it was because the carer needed the other person to be there either to help with his or her own personal care needs or for the social and emotional contact. For example, the 85-year-old mother of Pamela Wan had resisted attempts to provide her daughter with more independent accommodation ten years before. Her other daughter, who now provided considerable care for both of them, said that when this had been proposed her mother had been against it:

> 'Actually I think selfishly because she would be on her own... She said, "Oh, Pamela would never... cope with that, she'd be upset and all that." But it wouldn't, it wasn't Pamela that would be upset, it was my mum... She doesn't want to be on her own.'

The future of both older carers and older people with learning difficulties is, of course, an important and growing issue and yet it is one which both sides find very difficult to confront, even with the support and advice of a care worker. This difficulty may stem from a reluctance or unwillingness on the part of the carer, not just on the learning-disabled relative, to look ahead (see Ritchie & Richardson, 1989).

It is essential that people living with a family carer have carefully worked out plans that can be instituted if and when the caring relationship breaks down, as a result of death or ill-health. Without it, older people with learning difficulties, who now are increasingly likely to face life after the death of their principle carer, will experience increased trauma as they have to adjust both to the death of their closest relative, the loss of their principle carer, and a radical but unprepared-for change in their care and living arrangements. In one case, it had taken the social worker eight years to persuade an 83-year-old woman looking after her 53-year-old daughter to address the issue of future care. At the time of the interview, the daughter could not comprehend the possibility of her mother's death. In this case, the mother had always quietly assumed that her daughter would move into a local hostel when she could no longer provide care. Its closure left her devastated and with no idea about alternative provision.

Preparation for future care following the death of the carer, or when the carer can no longer cope with the task, is an extremely sensitive issue. Both the carer and their learning-disabled relative need support and information over a prolonged period. However, the gaps in service provision and the lack of a long-term relationship with a key worker, which was the experience of most family carers, means that this rarely happens. The current system, which concentrates resources on crisis intervention, means that neither families, service users nor service professionals can establish a long-term relationship based on trust, within which such sensitive issues can begin to be addressed.

Planning for the future

Some families had begun to consider possible future alternatives for care. Two-thirds of carers wanted their relative to remain in the family home with an input of formal service support. This option was being canvassed in particular by one parent, who cited several other cases where this had happened. However, in this and another instance, there was some uncertainty as to whether the tenancy of the house could be transferred to the service user, because only one transfer of tenancy could be made and that had occurred when the father had died and the mother took it over. Secondly, the social worker concerned was not optimistic that the necessary domiciliary support would be forthcoming, though in principle such an arrangement could be made.

Some family carers were unhappy with the alternative care arrangements available. One woman, who had cared for her brother since her mother's death and who had planned to relinquish care on her retirement, had not done so because she did not want him to go into a small group home, the most likely kind of placement available in the area: 'We were only supposed to look after him until we retired, then once that happened we were supposed to put him in a hostel. But of course there aren't any hostels any more. So I don't see any future at all except to look after him until he dies.'

Of course, had her brother been living in a hostel or one of the large hospitals, she would not have had any option about allowing him to go into an independent house and the evidence shows she would probably have been

pleased with it once he was safely settled (Walker *et al.*, 1993).

In one example, the principal carer of a woman who lived with her very frail mother said that she would like her sister to go into an older person's home. This was the service user who, through her mother, had had some contact with this service and seemed to be comfortable with it. This carer also said that she did not feel that a placement with other people with learning difficulties would be appropriate because: '[They] get on her nerves because she's a quiet person and they make a lot of noise. Some people... don't they, you know, with their disabilities and that?'

Planning is made more difficult, of course, by the uncertainty of when the need for formal care will arise. What can be done is for the range of options to be introduced to the parties concerned with, if possible, visits being made over time, as they should be with any resettlement. This means that people living with their families, like people who have been resettled, should have the opportunity for a periodic review to determine both immediate and longer term needs and goals. But only two out of the eight older people living with their families had had an IPP or equivalent in the recent past, and no relative had been involved in one of those.

A positive strategy for addressing the future care of older people with learning difficulties has been adopted in one of the Districts in the study. The District has identified between 30 and 40 individuals with learning difficulties who are being cared for by parents aged between 60 and 70 years of age. A Community Living Options Committee has been set up which pools all available service options for care and support in the area. This enables the service users, informal carers, and those involved in formal support, to consider the range of options which might become available so that decisions can be made before the sad occasion of someone's death or in advance of a breakdown in the caring arrangements because of changes in circumstances of the carer or the learning-disabled relative. Such arrangements can ease greatly the transition from family care to formal care. It is then important that the solutions offered are not as age-discriminatory as some of those offered to and available for the older people who have moved into the community from institutions. Help and support provided should be determined by the needs, abilities and preferences of the individual, not on the basis of age.

Conclusion

In this chapter, we have explored the long neglected but increasingly-pressing service issue of older people with learning difficulties. Our research has revealed considerable disparities between older and younger people with learning difficulties in the opportunities they are offered for participation in the everyday life of the community in which they live. We have identified age-discriminatory attitudes which, although often well-intentioned, may be denying older people chances for an improved quality of life. For the most part, the client group-orientated health and social services culture has not begun to address the emergence of this new user group and, as a result, they are falling between services for people with learning difficulties and those for older people. This double jeopardy is resulting in older people with learning difficulties being even more excluded and marginalised than those who fall neatly into the existing service-provision categories. Nor have policy-makers and service providers begun adequately to tackle the issue of the ageing of the family carers responsible for older people with learning difficulties, although one District in the North West had started to implement a positive strategy that contains elements of good practice.

The provision of small residential homes and individual support systems offers people with learning difficulties in the community more independent and less institutionalised models of care than those provided in residential homes for older people. Given that this type of provision has been shown to be appropriate across the spectrum of learning difficulty, there is no reason why it cannot be offered regardless of age. With appropriate staff training and flexibility, people with learning difficulties should be able to stay put as they age. In this respect, services for older people have much to learn from recent developments in the care of people with learning difficulties.

Chapter Five
Conclusion

This research started from the premise that there is widespread acceptance among policy-makers, service providers and people with learning difficulties and their families that ordinary housing within local communities provides the most appropriate setting for people with learning difficulties. This is not to neglect the very strong contrary views held by some people, most notably some parents of those living within institutions and some staff working with them (Allen *et al.*, 1990). The aim of this research was not to show that community living is better than institutional living, other research has already done that, but to examine the extent to which services were responding to different groups of people with learning difficulties living in the community on the basis of their needs and not according to particular categories of service or age, and to assess the quality of life that is thus offered to people with learning difficulties in the community.

Levels of service provision

The research described in this report confirmed that people with learning difficulties living in the community receive very different levels and types of service provision. People who had been resettled into formal care in the community generally had a key worker or other named person working regularly with them, most commonly in a supported living situation. However, very few had access to community learning disability services, such as respite facilities or domiciliary services, which were available to people living with their families. By contrast, people living with their families rarely had ongoing contact with, for example, a key worker who held a watching brief over their current and future needs. Their contact with the formal care sector was extremely passive, through day care and respite services, until and if a crisis arose.

Ex-hospital residents

The main explanation for the differences in service provision given to people with learning difficulties living in the community is that one group — ex-hospital residents — receives annual funding from the regional health authority on discharge to pay for their care throughout their lifetime. The importance of this cannot be over-emphasised. However, before a reallocation of financial resources between the three groups is seized on as a panacea for those inequalities which this research has demonstrated, two central issues need to be considered.

First, while those in the ex-hospital group have many advantages over the other two groups, (that is, those resettled from elsewhere without funding and those living with their families) there is still room for considerable improvement in their own quality of life. In particular, their ability to participate in community activities is restricted by inadequate and inflexible staffing levels which prevent them from leading an ordinary life in the most basic sense: being able to go where they want, when they want, on their own and not only in groups. Some service providers reported to us that resettlements were already being squeezed financially and that the packages of care were not as comprehensive for new resettlements as for old ones. This problem will be exacerbated, as the last people to be resettled will be those with the most complex needs. One purchasing manager said: 'There is increasingly less equity, for want of a better word, within the resettlement schemes that are up and running. So robbing Peter to pay Paul is increasingly not an option, because the schemes themselves… are running into deficit and we are having difficulty maintaining the same quality of service.'

Secondly, while the ex-hospital group have staff support dedicated to their needs, they do not have access to the other services available to other people with learning difficulties living in the community, especially day care services. They are usually excluded from such provision for one of three reasons. The first reason, which does have some justification, is that other people, namely people living with their families, should be given priority. This is based, it should be pointed out, both on the needs of the learning disabled person and on the needs of the carer for whom the day centre place provides essential daily 'respite' in the absence of little other domiciliary support. The other two reasons are, we believe, open to question. People living in a formal care setting are sometimes excluded from day centres because giving them access is regarded as making double provision. However, this is spurious: it is like saying that a child living in a foster home who goes to school receives double provision from the state. People living in supported living situations, like anyone else, need opportunities to have regular, organised activities outside the home.

The second questionable reason why this group is excluded is that the use of segregated facilities is seen as incompatible with the ordinary life model. As discussed in **Chapter Three**, there are very positive reasons why people with learning difficulties should be given opportunities to meet with other people with learning difficulties, should they so wish. Furthermore, an organised segregated service may be preferable to no provision outside the home. These arguments are closely bound up with the nature of day care provision. However, such a debate on the adequacy and appropriateness of day care provision is as valid for people living with their families as it is for people in formal care. If a particular model of care is good enough for one group, it is good enough for all. If it is inappropriate for one group then it is likely to be equally inappropriate for another. One service provider told us that demand for day centre places was now increasing from the ex-hospital group as some of the day centres were changing. Another was fearful that those places awarded to people living in supported accommodation might be jeopardised by a bulge in the number of younger people living at home who needed a place. One rationing mechanism being considered was to levy a charge on ex-hospital residents.

The main advantage that people who have been resettled into formal care have over those living with their families is that they have been fully assessed and an individual package of care has been provided. People being relocated from hospital have the added protection that, in order for the receiving authority to be given the dowry which accompanies each person they take responsibility for, the package of care has to meet the guidelines laid down in the *Model District Service*. Though in practice important compromises are made in this respect because the RHA needs to discharge people in order to run down and close the hospitals (Walker *et al.*, 1993), the care package provided does have to meet minimum specifications and to fit in generally with the principles of the Region's strategy of community services for people with learning difficulties. The hospital resettlement programme provides service users with a proper review of their needs and, in turn, forces on service providers a requirement to agree and provide an appropriate package of care. The hospital resettlement programme was guided by a Regional Implementation Group which had representation from the hospitals and the receiving districts and authorities. Each resettlement involved staff within the hospital, usually a resettlement worker, sometimes working with social work or nursing staff, who worked alongside staff from the receiving districts and local authorities.

Thus, as important as the money which accompanied the people moving out of hospital was the comprehensive, individual assessment of needs which was undertaken and the high profile which the hospital resettlement programme inevitably received, given the imminent closure of the hospitals and the need to develop community services to allow the reintegration of large numbers of people with learning difficulties back into the community.

Moving from family care

The resettlement of people from hostels and from the family home was quite different. The closure of hostels and the consequent resettlements, which in themselves represented a major achievement for the local authorities concerned (400 people in Greater Manchester and Lancaster moved out of hostels to supported living between 1990 and 1992), had to be achieved without any new funding. The move from family care to formal care tends to take place not as part of

a planned resettlement programme but in response to a family crisis, normally when family care breaks down. The exceptions were two people who had very limited learning difficulty and needed very little support to live independently. Once having been assessed and having been accepted solely as the responsibility of the formal care sector, the individuals concerned received a package of care not dissimilar in type, though at a lower level, than that provided for people in the ex-hospital group.

The big gap in the level and type of service provision occurs between people in formal care and those living with their families. The people in the family group were much less likely than those in formal care to have had either an assessment as provided for under the *NHS and Community Care Act, 1990* or to have had an IPP. A higher proportion in this group than the others had never had an IPP or had not had one in the previous six months. While most had a regular day centre place and occasional respite provision, they had little other contact with service providers. Neither they, nor their carers, received any ongoing support from the learning disability services. This means that there was no regular assessment of their care and support needs nor any planning for the future.

Some carers complained that they had to fight for all the services they received. Some were critical of the inability of the formal service sector to meet their care needs and were very concerned at the closure or threatened closure of day centres or respite services. Some service providers admitted that, in some areas, full-time day-centre provision could no longer be guaranteed. An increasing number of authorities are now levying charges for these essential services. One carer showed her frustration in the interview: 'In this area, I'll tell you this now, there's a lot of people who are getting ready to say that's enough. If they start to cut the services any more, there's about twenty or thirty carers who are gonna say, "Right, social services, here's twenty people for you, look after 'em".'

The reasons for the different treatment of those in formal and informal care are understandable, most notably because of the resource implications of assessing and then endeavouring to meet the needs of a whole new group of people with learning difficulties. Community provision for ex-hospital residents has been met by a reallocation of existing resources from the regional health authority to local service providers. There is no similar new pot of money to cover the needs of those living with families. The total costs of all caring by families is hidden and almost entirely carried by the family members themselves and represents very considerable savings to the Exchequer (according to the British Medical Association, this amounts to **£33.9 billion per year** for *all* carers). But this care is provided often at great sacrifice to the family carers and at the expense of reduced choice and opportunities for those they are looking after.

Service provision for people with learning difficulties should be based on individual needs, not on their particular service background. We have previously argued that the lives of people with learning difficulties in formal care would be enhanced by the use of domiciliary and peripatetic services, and even in the right circumstances, day centre or other similar daytime placement (Walker *et al.*, 1993). The situation of people living with their families is obviously different, not least because the needs and preferences of their carers must also be taken into account. Daytime and occasional respite care is extremely important for carers. However, it is important that the placement is suitable for the service user also. It should be more than

just somewhere to go outside the home. It should offer opportunities and new experiences which the family carer is either unable or reluctant to provide.

In one of the group interviews held with service users in a day centre, one respondent who was living with his family said that he wanted 'to be resettled into the community'. This comment, notable first for his use of service terminology, is also significant because he did not currently feel as if he was in the community — even though obviously he was in a physical sense. What the respondent wanted was, like most people in the general population, the opportunity to leave home and to live as independently as possible. An opportunity that is denied to most people living at home until the carer is unable or unwilling to continue. What is needed is a resettlement policy which enables those people living with their families who wish to 'move into the community' to move into supported or independent accommodation which they can feel is theirs.

To achieve this, family carers have to be confident about the quality of the placement. Inevitably, family carers' attitudes towards the formal sector are closely related to their previous experiences. A negative experience, no matter how long ago, can make them reluctant to get involved with the formal sector again. It may also be reliant on close contact with a key worker to ensure that they are familiar with the available options. This is particularly, but not only, important for older people with learning difficulties whose family carer, usually a parent, is also getting older and whose ability to care in the future is in doubt. However, policy-makers should not fall into the traditional 'casualty' mentality of social service providers (Walker, 1989) and leave planning for a more independent model of living until after the family arrangement has broken down. Leaving home, for people with learning difficulties, ideally should be as natural a step as it is for other members of the community. The only difference is that in their case support and care systems need to be put in place. Local authorities are now required to consider carers under the *Carers Recognitional Services Act, 1995*. However, in the past some family carers have proved resistant to separate assessments for the people they are caring for (Turner *et al.*, 1995). Nonetheless, the realisation of the aspirations of both parties is important for the quality of life of people with learning difficulties and their family carers.

The need to plan for future care is particularly acute for older people living with their families as an increasing number of carers themselves are well into advanced old age. If nothing is done until after the caring relationship has broken down, possibly on the death of the carer, then the service user has to cope with two traumas: the loss of the person closest to them and a change in their living situation. The Community Living Options Committee, set up in one of the authorities in the study, provides a forum for future planning which, in principle, can provide continuity in the care of an older person with learning difficulty and avoid the crisis intervention that is more common on the death of the carer.

The involvement of an advocate, or assistance for the service user in self-advocacy, could help to break the ice on many of the issues which have been raised by this research, both for people living with their families and for those in formal care. Although self-advocacy and citizen-advocacy are growing movements nationally and although there are some effective groups in the North West region, they cover a tiny proportion of the population. No-one in the family group had an advocate, while only three of those in formal care did. Unfortunately, even in these cases, the

advocacy system was not working terribly well. Care workers reported that the contact was not consistent and in one case the advocate had not been seen for several months. In the medium term, service providers should examine what can be done to establish and develop advocacy groups and to broaden their coverage more widely. One authority launched a two-year county-wide advocacy project; some others discuss the need for advocacy in their community care plans. In the meantime, care workers have to be trained on the nature of their relationship with the service user, so that it is supportive and enabling. Key workers should be allocated to people living with their families to help them, over time, develop care plans which reflect both sets of interests.

Older people with learning difficulties

In the post-War period, service providers have gradually adapted to the growing number of people with learning difficulty surviving into adulthood. A new challenge is now presenting itself in the form of increasing numbers living into older age. This is a challenge which services are only slowly addressing. The ageing of the learning disabled population has important implications for the concept of normalisation, which is based on the premise that this group should share in life experiences of the wider community. However, the limitations of the normalisation concept and putting it into operation are easily demonstrated with regard to older people with learning difficulties. Unless the stereotyping which affects service provision for all older people is challenged, then the goals set for older people with learning difficulties and the service responses offered will be restricted by the limited opportunities which are offered and the discriminatory attitudes which affect the social standing of all older people in the community.

The study found that staff working with older people with learning difficulties tend to stereotype them, with the result that the model of care adopted is usually based on assumptions of dependence not independence. Many care workers assumed that older people led sedentary lives, went out less than younger people, had less friends and that therefore less effort needed to be made to develop activities and foster integration of this group with the wider community. To the extent that these characteristics are a feature of older people's lives, they are, generally, not there out of choice but merely reflect the enforced social isolation of many older people (Tunstall, 1966; Walker, 1995a) As a result, care workers were less likely to believe that it was important to teach older people new skills and they believed, incorrectly on the basis of research evidence, that it was harder, if not impossible, for older people to develop new skills. These quite common views were in stark contrast to the very significant progress that many older people make in community living skills when they move out of hospital, often after decades of incarceration, which were reported in **Chapter Four** and in our previous research (Walker *et al.*, 1993). Such negative attitudes are also quite contrary to some of the experiences found among the older people in the study who were living with their families. There, we found several examples of the caring role being reversed: the learning disabled person was acquiring new skills and responsibilities in order to look after their own 'carer'.

The attitudes of care staff are quite consistent with formal service-provision for older people, which has been based on the idea of a service continuum — progressing from domiciliary to residential care. This carries an in-built assumption of the inevitability of decline and is ageist in conception, but also, it is contrary to many developments in service-provision for people with learning difficulties. In practical terms, it means that residential care is now considered as an appropriate option for an older person with learning difficulty, where it would not be deemed so for younger people (Walker *et al.*, 1996). One district purchaser reported that, although special permission had to be sought from the RHA to resettle people from hospital (though not from a community setting) to a residential care home (contrary to the guidelines in the *Model District Service*), it was now generally accepted that nursing home provision could be used: 'There is a small number of people who are going into nursing-home settings... [They] tend to be very elderly, who, if they were in the main population... would be accommodated in that type of resource.'

The danger with this view is that, as resources are increasingly squeezed, residential homes will be seen as a less expensive alternative to providing the enhanced support necessary to enable someone to stay at home — just as they are for the wider population of older people. In both cases, community care is not a cheap option if it is to genuinely improve the quality of life of both those in need of care and their families.

Lack of structured daytime activities is a problem for all people with learning difficulties; however, it was particularly acute for older people in this study. In practice, day centres are geared towards younger people, both because of their allocation policies and the activities which take place; some FE colleges discriminate against older people.

On the other side of the service divide, older people's services, which tend to cater mainly for the very elderly population, have little experience of people with learning difficulties and are often reluctant to take them. This leaves oider people with learning difficulties falling between two stools, nominally the responsibility of both sectors but in practice benefiting little or not at all from either. The majority of care workers interviewed said that the general level of services for older people was poor or very poor and yet several reported the closure of appropriate facilities in the recent past. The situation is unlikely to improve as social services budgets come under increasing pressure.

The ageing of the population of people with learning difficulties has other important implications for the nature and structure of service provision. Currently, learning disability services and services for older people are quite separate and there is very little overlap between the two. This can lead to 'double jeopardy', whereby older people with learning difficulties are inadequately served by both sets of services, as described above. However, perhaps even more important, is the philosophical difference between the two service sectors. The development of services for older people has not been accompanied by the same kind of debates about principles that have taken place in the learning difficulties field. By contrast, while there has been considerable rhetoric about enabling older people to stay in their homes or to live with their families, and there is some, very limited, financial help to assist them to do this, the number of older people in residential care has continued to grow and the levels of domiciliary support necessary to prevent this have failed to keep pace with demand (Walker, 1985; Schorr, 1992; Walker, 1995b).

The different principles underpinning service provision for older people and those with learning difficulties are usually implemented by the same health and social services agencies. Yet they imply very different forms and levels of service delivery and user rights. The survival of people with learning difficulties

into older age and their large-scale relocation into the community is beginning to expose these philosophical dilemmas: in service terms, are they older people or people with learning difficulties?

The research findings reported here show that many age-discriminatory stereotypes are now creeping into learning disability services. If these are not swiftly and comprehensively challenged, the opportunities and advantages that should be offered to older people with learning difficulties living in the community, some after long years of institutionalisation, will be limited merely on account of their age and not because of their abilities or, indeed inclinations. Thus, those ageist assumptions which prevail in much of the care of non-disabled older people will create even greater dependency among older people with learning difficulties. As a result, this group will not be able to benefit from the more creative and practical support that has allowed some younger people to obtain and retain a degree of independence following relocation from an institution. Such ageist attitudes and policies in service provision are restricting the extent to which older people with learning difficulties are able to benefit from the ordinary life model that is regarded widely as being entirely appropriate for their younger counterparts.

Key developments in service provision for people with learning difficulties

The model of care for people with learning difficulties is being transformed. In the North West the long-stay mental handicap hospitals are being closed. There has also been an active programme to run down hostel provision. Two authorities in our study predicted that they would have no hostel provision within their boundaries within two years. Others had similar ambitions but were concerned that their hostel closure programme would be curtailed because of a lack of funds. This institutional provision is being replaced mainly by supported living in ordinary housing in local communities.

The most obvious benefit of this policy shift has been felt by the people who have moved into ordinary community settings. However, there have been other advantages. First, the care and support of people with learning difficulties have received considerable attention and priority. There is also no doubt that devolving the money released by the closure of the hospitals has enabled some important developments in community services for people with learning difficulties in the North West and elsewhere (NW Region Review Working Group, 1989; Knapp *et al.*, 1992). The dowry, which is made by the Region to the receiving authority to meet the cost of care of individuals after resettlement, provides an important injection of new money essential for new community service developments. Needless to say, the pace at which that money comes on stream and the level of payment (which has fluctuated over the years) are crucial variables which determine the rate at which new facilities can be put in place and the quality of service which can be offered.

The need to protect the interests of people living with their families at a time when resettlement from hospital and hostels is receiving priority is stressed by the House of Commons Social Services Committee (1985): 'If the presently uneven balance is not redressed, all energies will be bent on providing services for people coming out of hospital, only to find equal pressure to use those facilities coming from people not currently in hospital.'

The *Model District Service* itself stressed that improved community provision is necessary for all people with learning difficulties, not least to eliminate the demand for new admissions to hospitals from families. The extent to which they have benefited in practical and direct terms from the shift of resources and effort from institutional to community care is very limited in the short and medium term. As people who have been resettled die, so other people living in the community can take their places in supported accommodation. In some areas, support services for all people with learning difficulties have been merged under one structure. This has led to greater equalisation of provision for those in formal care, for example, with regard to staffing levels, which address some of the disparities between the ex-hospital and community group discussed in **Chapter Two**. In four of the authorities in the study, the dowry payments are used exclusively to sustain the ex-hospital residents, which disappointed some service providers who had hoped the money could be used to develop new services, such as supported employment. In the fifth authority, ten per cent of the resettlement money is creamed off by the local authority to fund learning disability services to everyone in the community.

There is an extremely important management issue involved here. On the one hand, local health and social services should be aiming to provide an equal level of service provision to all on the basis of need. On the other hand, those involved in the resettlement process are extremely anxious that the packages of care and support which are agreed on discharge are not diluted over the years. Families, in particular, are extremely concerned about the long-term prospects for care of their learning-disabled relatives (Walker *et al.*, 1993), a fear which is quite justified given the pressure under which social services departments in particular work.

Some policy officers indicated in discussion with us that they had hoped that improvement in the independent living skills of ex-hospital residents after the move into the community would lead to a reduction in the level of support required. One Principal Officer said: 'Services haven't been able to grow away from that... I think we made the assumption that people would "get better" and staff would move on to do other things. That hasn't happened.'

One respondent attributed this to staff inertia or conservatism: 'Some staff get a little bit protective of the people they have worked with for a while. Maybe those who are looked after for 24 hours could manage with 15 or 10 hours in some cases.'

The reality is not so straightforward. While our previous research found that packages of care seldom changed after resettlement (for the better or for the worse), this might be due to the fact that changes may not be appropriate because, for example, growing independence may require more support (though less care). Thus, the amount of support may not change, while the nature of that support might do. In addition, the opportunities for individuals to move on to less supportive settings are extremely limited because of the narrow range of options currently available.

The financial pressures on services for those resettled from hospital are likely to get worse. All the senior personnel interviewed for the study admitted that the needs of those left in the hospitals were among the most complex. In particular, they are more likely to display challenging behaviour or have physical disabilities, as well as severe learning difficulties. They will often require specially-adapted accommodation, which is difficult to secure, as well as higher staffing. Placing people with challenging behaviours in

ordinary housing can succeed, but only if there are sufficient well-trained staff (Emerson, 1992), which of course increases costs and therefore may lead to an overall reduction in the number of placements. This effect is not unique to services in the North West (Link, ITV, 18.12.94). For this reason, families looking after people with complex needs may find it more difficult to secure a permanent full-time placement than will those whose relative requires lower levels of care and support.

The decentralisation of the 'Region'

Resettlement policy in the North West Health Region has been co-ordinated by the Regional Health Authority. It proved to be an effective advocate for change in service provision for people with learning difficulties and worked with receiving health districts and social services departments to ensure implementation of their ambitious policy objectives. The Region rightly earned itself a reputation as promoting needs-led and user-led services (CMH, 1982). This has had a dramatic effect both on the quantity and quality of placements for people who were relocated from hospital. One of the main hospitals scheduled for closure in 1996 was alone in being commended in a recent Values into Action report for not slowing up on resettlements after they were granted Trust status (Collins, 1993). The Regional Health Authority and various jointly-controlled policy-making bodies (Joint Strategy Group) were instrumental in setting up and endeavouring to maintain quality standards for all those resettled under the 'dowry' system. However, it must be said that the Region's power to enforce changes in provision after resettlement has been called into question (Walker *et al.*, 1993).

Recent changes in national policy have put a strain on the coherence of Regional policy.

First, the changing role and structure of the Regional Health Authorities, together with key changes in personnel, has reduced the extent to which the Region wants or is able to control practice in local social services departments or district health authorities.

Secondly, when the purchaser/provider split was introduced into the health and social services by the *NHS and Community Care Act*, most of those previously working in service development and operational management tended to opt to work on the provider side. This has resulted in new personnel being appointed to act as purchasers of services and there has been some concern, particularly among those engaged in resettlement from long-stay hospitals, that they do not share the Region's long-standing commitment to small-scale provision.

The purchaser/provider split was identified by managers as one of the factors which was forcing down staff costs, the largest element in health and social services budgets. Staff who currently work for statutory service providers are employed on conditions and wages which are negotiated at a national level. Independent-sector providers have no such agreements and therefore have lower labour costs. One senior manager of a statutory provider reported that current levels of pay for staff working in his supported settings would have to be re-negotiated if they were to compete in the mixed economy. This and our previous research has shown that a high proportion of care workers have no formal training or experience of working with people with learning difficulties. If labour costs are driven down still further, then it will be extremely difficult to attract and retain good quality staff. Furthermore, complex skills are needed to carry out a supportive role which is meant to enable people with learning difficulties to participate in their communities rather than be 'cared' for in isolated houses. The need for well-motivated, well-trained staff is paramount. In their absence, the quality of the service will be in jeopardy.

The encouragement of private and voluntary sector involvement in the provision of care under the *NHS and Community Care Act*, 1990 has led to an increase in the number of service providers. However, more providers does not necessarily mean greater diversity or greater choice. Providers have to compete both on cost and quality; and many people working in services are worried that purchasers are more concerned with the former than the latter. Furthermore, from our discussions with purchasers it was not clear that there were always effective mechanisms in place to monitor properly the very many, sometimes one-off schemes, that have been commissioned. The model of small group supported living — in the public, private and voluntary sectors — must be accompanied by effective and independent monitoring procedures, in which people with learning difficulties play a central part.

Developments in the learning difficulty field have been at the forefront of the creation of a user-led model of care. Many important achievements have been made. Increasing numbers of people with learning difficulties are now living in ordinary housing, with support, in the community. Steps have been taken to offer them an increasing range of choices and opportunities as well as to foster independence.

The resettlement of people out of hospital in the North West has provided an impetus and a focus for better services for all people with learning difficulties. Inevitably, inequalities arise. The challenge for service providers is to tackle this by aspiring to provide the best models of good practice for *all*, and *not* to opt to improve the lot of the worst off by diluting provision given to those who are more fortunate in service terms. Some examples of good practice have been reported earlier. But the achievement of quality services and a good quality of life for *all* people with learning difficulties, regardless of their service background and regardless of their age, will depend on a continuing commitment to respond to each person's individual needs and not fall into the trap of looking only at their service history. In this way it may be possible to create fair service shares for all people with learning difficulties.

References

Abraham, C. (1989): Supporting People With a Mental Handicap in The Community: a social psychological perspective. *Disability, Handicap & Society*, **4** (2).

Allen, P., Pahl, J. & Quine, L. (1990): *Care Staff in Transition*. HMSO.

Ashton, D. (1995): *Survey of Supported Employment in the North West*. Clitheroe: NWTDT.

Audit Commission (1995): *Local Authority Performance Indicators, Vol. 1*. HMSO.

Bayley, M. (1994): An Eye for Detail. *Community Care*, 10 September.

Belbin, E. & Belbin, R, M. (1972): *Problems in Adult Retraining*. Heinneman.

Belbin, R. M. (1965): *Training Methods for Older Workers*. Paris: OECD.

Berthoud, R., Lakey, J. & McKay, S. (1993): *The Economic Problems of Disabled People*. Policy Studies Institute.

Booth, T., Simons, K. & Booth, W. (1990): *Outward Bound: Relocation and community care for people with learning difficulties*. OUP.

Briggs, A. & Oliver, J. (Eds.) (1988): *Caring: Experiences of Looking after Disabled Relatives*. Routledge.

Brown, H. (1994): What Price Theory if You Cannot Afford the Bus Fare: Normalisation and leisure services for people with learning disabilities. *Health and Social Care in the Community*, **1** (2).

Brown, H. & Smith, S. (1992): *Normalisation: A Reader for the Nineties*. Routledge.

Brown, S. & Wistow, G. (1990): *The Roles and Tasks of Community Mental Handicap Teams*. Avebury.

Bulmer, M. (1987): *The Social Basis of Community Care*. Allen & Unwin.

Carter, J. (1988): *Creative Day-Care for Mentally Handicapped People*. Blackwell.

Chappell, A.L. (1992): Towards a Sociological Critique of the Normalisation Principle. *Disability, Handicap and Society*, **7** (1), pp35–52.

Chappell, A.L. (1994): A Question of Friendship: community care and the relationships of people with learning difficulties. *Disability, Handicap and Society*, **9** (4), pp419–434.

CMH (1982): *Planning for Change*. London: Campaign for the Mentally Handicapped.

Collins, J. (1992): *When Eagles Fly: A report on the resettlement of people with learning difficulties from long-stay hospitals.* London: Values Into Action.

Collins, J. (1993): *The Resettlement Game: Policy and procrastination in the closure of mental handicap hospitals.* London: Values Into Action.

Conroy, J. & Bradley, V. (1985): *The Pennhurst Longitudinal Study: A Report of Five Years' Research and Analysis.* Temple University Developmental Disabilities Centre, Boston, Human Services Research Institute.

Davies, A., Murray, J. & Flynn, M. (1993): *Normal Lives? The financial circumstances of people with learning disabilities.* Manchester: NDT.

Doyal, L. & Gough, I, (1991): *A Theory of Human Need.* Macmillan.

Dybwad, G. (1962): Administrative and Legislative Problems in the Care of the Adult and Aged Mental Retarded. *American Journal of Mental Deficiency,* **66**, pp716–22.

Emerson, E. (1994): Self Injurious Behaviour: An overview of recent trends in Epidemiological and behavioural research. *Mental Handicap Research,* **5** (1).

Emerson, E. & Hatton, C. (1994): *Moving Out – The impact of relocation from hospital to community on the quality of life of people with learning difficulties.* HMSO.

Farnham-Diggory, S. (1978): *Learning Disabilities.* Fontana.

Fatimilehin, I. & Nadirshaw, Z. (1994): A Cross Cultural Study of Parental Attitudes and Beliefs about Learning Disability. *Mental Handicap Research,* **7** (3).

Felce, D. & Perry, J. (1995): Quality of Life: Its definition and measurement. *Research in Developmental Disabilities,* **16** (1), pp51–74.

Felce, D. & Toogood, S. (1988): *Close to Home.* Kidderminster: BIMH.

Finch, J. & Groves, D. (Eds.) (1983): *A Labour of Love: Women, work and caring.* Routledge.

Flynn, M. (1989): *Independent Living For Adults with Mental Handicap: A place of my own.* Cassell.

Flynn, M. (1994): *Taking a Break: Liverpool's respite services for adult citizens with learning disabilities.* Manchester: NDT.

Garvey, K. & Stenfert Kroese, B. (1991): Social Participation and Friendships of People with Learning Difficulties: A review. *The British Journal of Mental Subnormality,* **37**, Part 1, (72).

George, M. (1994): *Finding a Future.* Community Care, 3–9 November.

Glendinning, C. (1984): *The Financial Circumstances of Informal Carers.* York: SPRU.

Glendinning, C. (1992): *The Costs of Informal Care.* HMSO.

Grant, G. & Nolan, M. (1993): Informal Carers: Sources and concomitants of satisfaction. *Health and Social Care in the Community,* **1** (3).

Grant, L. (1995): *Disability and Debt: The experience of disabled people in debt.* Sheffield Citizens' Advice Bureau Debt Support Unit.

Health and Social Services Committee (1985): *Community Care.* HC-1, HMSO.

Hogg, J., Moss, S. & Cooke, D. (1988): *Ageing and Mental Handicap.* Croom Helm.

Jahoda, A., Cattermole, M. & Markova, I. (1990): Moving Out: An opportunity for friendship and broadening social horizons? *Journal of Mental Deficiency Research,* **34**, April.

Knapp, M. *et al.* (1992): *Care in the Community: Challenge and Demonstration.* Aldershot: Ashgate.

Korman, N. & Glennerster, H. (1990): *Hospital Closure.* Open University Press.

Liu, B. C. (1976): *Quality of Life Indicators in US Metropolitan Areas: A Statistical Analysis.* New York: Praeger Publications.

Maaskant, M., Kessels, A., Frederiks, C., Haveman, M., Lantman, H., Urlings, H., & Stermans, F. (1994): *Care Dependence and Policy Purposes.* Paper given at Older People with Development Disabilities Conference, Dublin, April.

Martin, J. & White, A. (1988): *The Financial Circumstances of Disabled Adults Living In Private Households.* HMSO (OPCS Disability Surveys, Report 2).

Martin, J., Meltzer, H. & Eliot, D. (1988): *Prevalence of Disability Among Adults.* HMSO.

Morris, J. (1993): *Independent Lives: Community Care and Disabled People.* Macmillan.

Morris, J. (1993a): *Community Care or Independent Living.* York: Joseph Rowntree Foundation/Community Care.

NWRHA (1982): *A Model District Service.* Manchester: NWRHA.

NWRHA (1991): Paper circulated to a meeting of the Regional Implementation Group, September.

NWRHA (1992): *Caught In the Competence Trap.* Manchester: NWRHA.

North West Region Review Working Group (1989): *Shared Proposals for Shared Problems: A joint health & social services review of the financial and planning arrangements for the implementation of the mental handicap strategy in the North West.* Manchester: NWRHA.

NWTDT (1994): *A Strategy for the 90s.* Manchester: NWTDT.

O'Brien, J. (1985): *A Guide to Personal Futures Planning.* Atlanta: Responsive Systems Associates.

Oppenheim, C. (1993): *Poverty, the Facts.* CPAG.

People First (1994): *Outside but not Inside… YET!* People First.

Porterfield, J. (1988): Promoting Opportunities For Employment. In: D. Towell (Ed.), *An Ordinary Life In Practice: Developing comprehensive community-based services for people with learning disabilities.* King's Fund.

Qureshi, H. & Walker, A. (1989): *The Caring Relationship.* Macmillan.

Richardson, A. & Ritchie, J. (1989): *Developing Friendships: Enabling people with learning difficulties to make and maintain friends.* London: PSI/SCPR.

Richardson, A. & Ritchie, J. (1990): Developing Friendships. In: T. Booth (Ed.) *Better Lives: Changing services for people with learning difficulties.* Sheffield University: Social Services Monographs.

Schorr, A. (1992): *The Personal Social Services: An Outside View.* York: Joseph Rowntree Foundation.

Simons, K. (1995): *My Home, My Life.* Values in Action.

Smull, M. & Burke Harrison, S. (1992): *Supporting People with Severe Reputations in the Community.* Virginia: National Association of State Directors of Developmental Disabilities.

Social Services Inspectorate (1994): *Caring for Quality in Day Services.* Department of Health/SSD, HMSO.

Stenfert Kroese, B. & Fleming, I. (1992): Staff Attitudes and Working Conditions in Community Based Group Homes for People with a Mental Handicap. *Mental Handicap Research,* **5** (1).

Sutcliffe, J. & Simons, K. (1993): *Self-advocacy and Adults with Learning Difficulties: Contexts and debates.* The National Institute of Adult Continuing Education.

Sweeney, D. P. & Wilson, T. Y. (1979): *Double Jeopardy: The plight of aging and aged developmentally disabled persons in Mid-America – a research monograph.* University of Michigan, Ann Arbor.

Taylor, P. E. & Walker, A. (1994): *The Ageing Workforce: Employers' attitudes towards older people.* Work, Employment and Society, **8** (4) pp569–591.

Townsend, P. (1981): Elderly People with Disabilities. In: A. Walker with P. Townsend (Eds.) *Disability in Britain.* Martin Robertson.

Todd, S., Shearn, J. & Felce, D. (1994): *Troubles of Time and Identity: The experiences of parents with co-resident adult offspring with learning disabilities.* Paper presented at 5th International Round Table on Ageing and Developmental Disabilities, Dublin.

Tunstall, J. (1966): *Old and Alone.* Routledge.

Turner, S., Sweeney, D. & Hayes, L. (1995): *Developments in Community Care for Adults with Learning Difficulties: A review of 1993/94 community care plans.* HMSO.

Twigg, J., Atkin, K. & Perring, C. (1990): *Carers and Services: A review of research.* HMSO.

Twigg, J. & Atkin, K. (1993): *Carers Perceived.* OUP.

Walker, A. (1980): The Social Creation of Poverty and Dependency in Old Age. *Journal of Social Policy,* **9** (1), pp49–75.

Walker, A. (1981): Community Care and the Elderly in Great Britain: Theory and practice. *International Journal of Health Services,* **11** (4), pp541–557.

Walker, A. (1982): *Unqualified and Underemployed: Handicapped young people and the labour market.* Macmillan.

Walker, A (1982a): Dependency and Old Age. *Social Policy and Administration,* **16** (2), pp116–137.

Walker, A. (1985): *The Care Gap*. Local Government Information Unit.

Walker, A. (1989): Community Care. In: M. McCarthy (Ed.) *The New Politics of Welfare*. Macmillan, pp205-225.

Walker, A. (1995a): *Maintaining Social Integration in An Ageing Society*. First Liz McKean Memorial Lecture, University of North London.

Walker, A. (1995b): *Half a Century of Promises*. Counsel and Care.

Walker, A., Walker, C. & Ryan, T. (1996): Older People with Learning Difficulties Leaving Institutional Care: A Case of Double Jeopardy. *Ageing and Society*, **16** (2), pp125–150.

Walker, C. (1993): *Managing Poverty: The Limits of Social Assistance*. Routledge.

Walker, C., Ryan, T. & Walker, A. (1993): *Quality of Life After Resettlement for People with Learning Disabilities*. Manchester: NWRHA.

Walker, P. & Racino, J. A. (1993): Being with People: Support and support strategies. In: J.A. Racino, P. Walker, S. O'Connor & S.J. Taylor (Eds.) *Housing Support and Community:*

Choices and strategies for people with disabilities. London, Baltimore: Paul H. Brookes.

Ward, L. (1990): A Programme for Change: Current issues in services for people with learning difficulties. In: T. Booth (Ed.) *Better Lives: Changing services for people with learning difficulties*. University of Sheffield, Social Services monographs: Research in Practice.

Warr, P. B. (1993): Age and Employment. In: M. Dunnette, *et al.*, (Eds.) *Handbook of Industrial and Organizational Psychology*, Vol. 4. Palo Alto: Consulting Psychologists Press.

Wolfensberger, W. (1972): *The Principle of Normalization in Human Services*, Toronto: National Institute on Mental Retardation.

Zarb, G. (1991): Creating a Supportive Environment: Meeting the needs of people who are ageing with a disability. In: M. Oliver (Ed.) *Social Work: Disabled people and disabling environments*. Jessica Kingsley.

Zarb, G. & Oliver, M. (1993): *Ageing with a Disability: What do they expect after all these years?* Joseph Rowntree Foundation.

Appendix One

European Network on Intellectual Disabilities and Ageing (ENIDA)

A subsidiary element of this project was the establishment of a pilot project to gather information on service provision for older people with learning difficulties in other European countries. In partnership with the Fondation de France, in Paris, an application was made to the European Commission to fund an initial meeting of a network of researchers and practitioners in the field of ageing and learning difficulties. After considerable internal delays, the Commission agreed to a grant of 15,000 Ecu, which the Foundation supplemented with 5,000 Ecu. As a result, an initial meeting of the network was held in Paris on 15 December 1994. Some 20 researchers and practitioners were present at the meeting, representing ten European Union countries. After considerable discussion, which focused primarily on differences in terminology between countries, it was agreed, in principle, to establish a network.

The Network has the following aims:

- To define priorities for scientific and field research, assist in the co-ordination of existing European research projects and help develop new transnational projects.

- To develop effective communication between practitioners and researchers, referring needs for new research, as defined by European practitioners, towards appropriate research teams and — on the other hand — referring requests for concrete feedback from researchers toward practitioners.

- To work within the supranational cultural identity of the European Union, and to explore the various national approaches to research as well as practice in the realm of ageing and intellectual disability, in order to develop mutual understanding.

- To disseminate viable extant information on ageing and intellectual disability (written documentation, video tapes) to social scientists and practitioners working in the realm of ageing as well as that of disability to advise authors on how to get their work published, and to centralise bibliographical references.

- To share the findings of new research with all the member states represented in the European Network on Intellectual Disability and Ageing.

The Sixth International Round Table on Older Persons with Mental Retardation (Special Interest Group of the IASSMD), in Vienna 27-28 April 1995, provided the opportunity to formally inaugurate the network. Thus ENIDA was born out of this project, with Nancy Breitenbach (Fondation de France) elected as President and Alan Walker as Vice-President. The inaugural meeting included representatives from Austria, Belgium, France, Germany,

Ireland, Italy, The Netherlands, Spain, Sweden and the UK. Subsequently researchers from Finland and Portugal have joined the network.

A key function of ENIDA is to exchange information on research and practice with regard to older people with learning difficulties between European Union countries and this process is now underway. An application has been made to BIOMED 2 in order to place the network on a sound financial footing. A book comparing services in different European Union countries is planned.

Appendix Two

Characteristics of the Sample

Table 1   Sample by Local Authority

L.A.	Ex-hospital	Community	Family	Total
Blackburn	10	6	7	23
Manchester	11	5	5	21
Oldham	13	7	7	27
Rochdale	16	4	4	24
Salford	10	8	7	25
Total	60	30	30	120

Table 2   Profile of People With Learning Difficulties In The Sample, By Age

Age	Ex-hospital	Community	Family	Total
<30	–	4	12	16
30–39	13	3	7	23
40–49	18	2	3	23
50–59	16	7	4	27
60–69	10	12	4	26
70+	3	2	–	5
Total	60	30	30	120

Table 3   **Sample by Gender**

	Ex-hospital	Community	Family	Total
Female	26	10	17	53
Male	34	20	13	67
Total	60	30	30	120

Competencies

There were considerable differences in the level of competencies of the three groups.

Overall, the community group showed the highest level of competencies and the ex-hospital group the lowest. Those living with their families tended to have a more even spread.

Table 4   **Self-Care Skills, Such As Washing, Dressing and Eating (%)**

Level of Competence	Ex-hospital	Community	Family
Can manage:			
Without help	48.3	86.7	73.3
With some help	30.0	6.7	3.3
With help	21.7	6.7	23.4
Total number	60.0	30.0	30.0

Table 5   **Competence In The Area of Understanding and Communication (%)**

Level of Competence	Ex-hospital	Community	Family
Independent	25.0	60.0	50.0
Semi-independent	23.3	16.7	16.7
Dependent	51.7	23.3	66.6
Total number	60.0	30.0	30.0

Table 6 Competence In The Area of Handling Money and Making Choices With Money (%)

Level of Competence	Ex-hospital	Community	Family
Independent	6.7	23.3	13.3
Semi-independent	38.4	43.3	36.6
Dependent	55.0	33.3	50.0
Total number	60.0	30.0	30.0

Table 7 Competence In Being Able To Participate In Community Activities Without Support (%)

Level of Competence	Ex-hospital	Community	Family
Independent	13.3	46.7	10.0
Semi-independent	53.3	43.3	70.0
Dependent	33.3	13.0	20.0
Total number	60.0	30.0	30.0

Health and disability

Illness

There was no significant difference in the health of the ex-hospital and community groups. Just over one-third of both groups (ex-hospital 38.3%, community 36.7%) were said to have some kind of long-standing illness or condition. The family group reported a slightly lower figure with nearly one-quarter (23.3%) reporting health problems. In addition, two people in the family group were said to have eating disorders which gave considerable concern to the carers and professionals involved.

Medication

A slightly higher proportion of the ex-hospital group were receiving some form of long-term medication. The figures for both groups were high: for the ex-hospital group almost eight in ten were receiving long-term medication, for the community group seven out of ten were. The levels of medication for the family group were not collected. Of those who were on medication, 60% were receiving it because of what could be termed behavioural reasons. There was no significant difference between the two groups. Some 25% of each group were receiving anti-convulsants and 15% had medication for both behaviour and epilepsy.

Physical disability

There was a significant difference between the groups with regard to physical disability. Over half of the ex-hospital group (53.3%) were said to have some kind of physical disability, compared to just over one-third (36.6%) of the community group and one-quarter of the family group (23.3%). A fifth (21.7%) of the ex-hospital group had quite profound physical disabilities and were reliant on others for

Table 8 Challenging Behaviour Reported By Care Workers

	None	Moderate	Severe	Fluctuates	Total
Ex-hospital	41.7	20.0	26.6	11.7	60.0
Community	60.0	16.6	10.0	13.3	30.0

basic personal care. Only one person in the community group had such disabilities and this was true of three of the family group.

Challenging behaviour

The issue of challenging behaviour was pursued more rigorously among those who lived in formal supported settings. In the case of the family group, the definition of challenging behaviour was left very much to the carer. In interviews with support staff, challenging behaviour was defined as: *behaviour which may cause injury to him or herself or to others, behaviour which may require the intervention of staff or which may restrict his or her use of community facilities.*

Over half of the ex-hospital group (58.3%) were said to display some kind of challenging behaviour: 12 (40%) of the community group and eight of the family group were said to display such behaviour. Furthermore, in most of the people in the community group, their challenging behaviour was moderate, such as verbal abuse. The ex-hospital group tended to display more wide-ranging behaviours, such as violence to those around them and to property. This data was taken from descriptions of the episodes of such behaviours from care staff and unpaid carers. Paid care-staff were also asked to quantify such behaviour themselves. *Table 8* above indicates differences between the two groups.

Only one third of all those displaying any kind of challenging behaviour received extra help in the form of clinical psychology services, additional support teams or challenging behaviour teams.

The ex-hospital group were also said to display challenging behaviour more frequently. One-third did so on a daily or weekly basis, whereas only one person from the community group was said to display such behaviour so frequently. Such behaviour tends to have an adverse effect on other people since those who have been resettled from hospitals tend to live with others. Over one-third of the ex-hospital group (36.6%) were said to display behaviour which had a negative effect on fellow tenants, while under one-quarter (23.3%) of the community group did so. In five cases, all of whom had been resettled from hospital, staff reported that the behaviour was having a severe negative effect on others living in the same house.

Table 9 Profile of Informal Carers, By Age

Age	Number
40–49	7
50–59	7
60–69	6
70–79	8
80+	2
Total	30